BOUND
by hand

BOUND
by hand

OVER
20
BEAUTIFULLY
HANDCRAFTED
JOURNALS

Erica Ekrem

LARK
New York

New York

An Imprint of Sterling Publishing Co., Inc.
1166 Avenue of the Americas
New York, NY 10036

LARK CRAFTS and the distinctive LARK logo are registered trademarks of
Sterling Publishing Co., Inc.

ISBN 978-1-4547-1055-4

Distributed in Canada by Sterling Publishing Co., Inc.
c/o Canadian Manda Group, 664 Annette Street
Toronto, Ontario, Canada M6S 2C8
Distributed in the United Kingdom by GMC Distribution Services
Castle Place, 166 High Street, Lewes, East Sussex, England BN7 1XU
Distributed in Australia by NewSouth Books
45 Beach Street, Coogee, NSW 2034, Australia

For information about custom editions, special sales, and premium and corporate purchases, please contact
Sterling Special Sales at 800-805-5489 or specialsales@sterlingpublishing.com.

Manufactured in China

2 4 6 8 10 9 7 5 3 1

sterlingpublishing.com
larkcrafts.com

Illustrations by Alexis Seabrook throughout, Illustrations by Sue Havens on pages 5, 12, 14-16,
18-20, 23-29, Author Photo by Satya Curcio on page 152
Interior design by Lorie Pagnozzi
Cover design by Elizabeth Mihaltse Lindy

Contents

Introduction

Since the time I attended my very first bookbinding class almost a decade ago, I've met hundreds of bookbinders and have found there to be a certain kind of person that revels in the beauty of hand-bound books. Some bookbinders fall fast into friendship with one another while others seem to believe in contrasting approaches. Yet there is a distinct thread of similarity running through us—we love the look and feel, and the undeniable potential, of a hand-stitched book.

Our reasons are diverse. In this age of technology, it has become extraordinary to make something so ordinary with one's own hands. It has become distinctly easier to buy a handmade book than to source all the tools and materials and carve out the space and time to make one yourself. Yet we do it because it is empowering to create a book from scratch, even if it doesn't turn out perfect the first or tenth time. An imperfect book is still beautiful, perhaps because we're surrounded by machine-made goods that are so strictly rectangular or circular that we can't help but adore imperfection for its rarity and the subtle sense of anima that emanates from it. Or maybe we love handmade books purely for the possibility they suggest—a new beginning, a story waiting to be told, a miniature gallery ready to take form. And sometimes blank books help us make sense of our lives. Their ordered pages suggest a definite beginning and end and can help us to begin fresh, find closure, and, overall, make sense of thoughts, feelings, and life events that can often feel blurred or non-linear. We write, document, sketch, and practice creative expression to find the meaning of life, or to rewrite a way of living that would better serve ourselves and the world around us.

Perhaps the biggest reason we are drawn to handmade books is because we humans have been making and using them as tools for a very long time. Journaling in particular is an ancient practice. Relics of manuscripts have been found that date back to 56 AD in China. Some of my favorite examples of historical journals are the pillow books of tenth-century Japan. These private diaries were kept by women of the court and were inscribed with personal musings, poetry, short stories, and opinions they could not openly share during that time period. Modern memoirs, such as the diary of Anne Frank, have given us a glimpse into the ways in which one's inner life carries on and seeks inspiration despite immensely difficult circumstances faced in the outer world. Frank's private writings teach us compassion and help us to transform the world into one that celebrates diversity and tolerance.

In the twenty-first century, many of us have moved our diaries or writing to the Internet in the form of digital blogs or daily posts on social media. I admit that I too have found myself typing on a keyboard more often than putting my pen to the pages of my journal. However, there is something intrinsically human in the act of putting ink on paper. For me, writing in a journal seems to counterbalance the impersonality and sterility of high technology. When we make a mistake with the pen, we can't simply delete it as if it didn't exist. With our mistakes on paper, we get to face our humanity and become intimate with it again. We get to face the beautiful imperfections that make each of us unique. The same goes for the hand-bound book—even if you follow the instructions in this book word for word, using the same tools and identical materials listed here, your book is going to become an object of art that is uniquely yours.

Whoever you are and whatever your reason for loving handmade books, thank you for being here. In the following pages, you'll find projects for making a diverse range of books that will serve a variety of daily purposes. I will lead you step by step through folk-style bookbinding projects that you can make from a humble set of tools and common materials, some of which you can upcycle from thrift stores or even find at home. You don't have to be experienced in bookbinding to attempt these projects; these are everyday books for everyday folks. Whether you're new to the art of bookbinding or a seasoned binder, I offer this book as a resource for learning new techniques, fueling your creativity, and helping empower and express your uniquely authentic self.

You'll learn to make books to serve your occupation or hobby—builder, poet, or herbalist, for example. There are books you can put to use on a daily basis for note-taking, as a spiritual practice, and for keeping track of your favorite recipes. Some projects may challenge how you think of or identify with yourself, giving you the opportunity to connect with the artist, mystic, or alchemist archetype within you. You'll also learn new knots, ornamental weaving techniques, and how to dye handmade paper from a rainbow of ingredients found in your kitchen pantry. And if you are someone with a daily journaling practice, I've designed projects especially for you too.

Learning a new skill or technique can be awkward sometimes. If you find yourself challenged at any point while making your hand-bound book or while filling the pages within, I encourage you to step outside. Give yourself the gift of fresh air by taking a few deep breaths; then take a walk alongside plants or a nearby body of water to change the rhythm of your thinking. I promise you will feel different, something inside you will shift, and when you come back to your project it will seem a little or a lot less intimidating. If you enjoy collaboration, invite a family member or a circle of friends to your home and make books together. It is likely you will each have diverse strengths and skill sets to offer and can help one another out when needed, as well as enjoy the benefit of camaraderie during the process. The projects range in difficulty, with some a bit more challenging than others. I encourage you to try them all. If the first attempt doesn't work out, don't be afraid to try again. No matter your experience, start with the basics, such as a pamphlet-stitch variation; then build up to more complex multistitch bindings.

Throughout the book, you will explore a variety of book structures as well as try out nontraditional mate-rials that can be sourced from your home or from spe-cialty stores. Accompanying each project are prompts that relate to the theme or type of book you have made. I hope these will encourage you to dive deeper into yourself, to find clarity when needed, to embrace your imperfections, and to simply make a habit of putting your pen, or paintbrush, to paper more often.

No matter your reason for loving hand-bound books, my wish is that after thoroughly exploring the projects within, you'll find yourself to be a more experienced bookbinder with a beautifully imperfect library of your own making.

THE BASICS

SOURCING MATERIALS AND TOOLS

I'm a big supporter of reusing materials. I believe the more we reuse, the lower the impact we will have on the environment. Also, I think of it as a creative challenge: How much fun can I have while sourcing my materials, and can I make new relationships (with materials, people, nature, etc.) in the process?

When searching for materials and tools, I always look in this order first:

1. Home, especially my backyard and materials stash

2. Secondhand sources, such as thrift shops or salvaging leftover scraps from friends or factories

3. Local shops and specialty purveyors

4. Online shops or larger stores

When purchasing tools, I look for high-quality ones that will last a lifetime. My tools are often made of metal and wood. I try to avoid plastic tools or ones that might break after a few uses.

MATERIALS

The following is an introduction to the materials that you will use to build your hand-bound books. I encourage you to explore materials you haven't previously used, as well as work with your favorite ones in a new way.

Paper

Paper is the essential ingredient of most hand-bound books. Since there is an incredible variety of papers available today, I will highlight the types that I specifically use in this book.

WRITING OR TEXT-WEIGHT PAPER is a lightweight to medium-weight paper that is usually between 35 lb. and 80 lb. (52 and 120 grams per square meter, or gsm). It can easily be grouped

including handmade papers from all over the world, screen-printed papers, and classic marbled papers. The criteria for choosing a decorative paper are simple. Like writing paper, it should be strong yet flexible enough to fold without cracking. It should not flop over on itself and be so fragile that it is easily torn from the book.

HANDMADE PAPER is usually created from natural fibers and can lend your book a rustic, tactile quality. Often the edges of the paper are deckle, meaning they have an organic, raw edge as opposed to a straight, trimmed edge. When using handmade paper, I like to feature the deckle edge whenever possible. Handmade paper is wonderful for pages in the text block if its surface is smooth enough for writing; otherwise, it can be used as a decorative element like an end sheet, or as a page that features your watercolor art or other artistic renderings.

Handmade papers from all over the world are available for purchase at local art stores and online. Lokta paper, made from Daphne shrub bushes in Nepal, is one of the most versatile papers to work with and a great choice if you are new to bookbinding. It comes in a variety of colors, sheet sizes, and weights. Also consider seeking out and supporting papermakers in your area. They may be using fibers that are native to your environment and may offer a paper that will contribute a unique, local nuance to your bound book.

MIXED-MEDIA PAPERS are ideal choices for making books that will hold artwork. Art papers included in the projects in this book include watercolor paper and canvas paper. They are specifically

into four to eight sheets and folded into a signature, one of the folded units of papers that makes up the pages of the book. A group of all the total compiled signatures is called a text block. Ideally, the paper you choose will have a smooth, matte surface that will allow for a variety of writing utensils, such as a ballpoint pen, pencil, marker, or even a dip pen or fountain pen. Most importantly, it needs to be flexible enough to be folded without cracking and strong enough to be punched with an awl and to hold thread without easily tearing. Most of the writing paper used in this book is produced by machine.

DECORATIVE PAPER lends character to your book. It is most often used in the front and back of the book to line the inside covers and serve as protective end sheets before the first page in the signature and after the last page of the last signature. There is a wide range of decorative papers to choose from, designed to accept the additional fluid content of watercolors and paints. You might even consider gluing blank canvas paper to boards to make paintable canvas covers for your books.

WATERPROOF PAPER has been engineered with a special coating that will allow you to write in the rain, and it will tolerate light moisture. This paper is ideal for those who journal outdoors and those who prefer a hardier book that will withstand the natural elements.

CARDSTOCK is a thick paper primarily used for single pages in a recipe book or scrapbook. It usually has a weight of 80 lb. (120 gsm) or more and can be folded one sheet at a time. Many of the projects in this book use cardstock to make templates and punching guides.

Leather

A leather-bound book is both beautiful and utilitarian. Leather as a cover material has withstood the test of time and lengthens the life span of the pages by protecting the text block from the elements and from general wear and tear. In the projects in this book, I recommend specific weights of leather that will work best for the particular structure of book you will be making. Leather thickness is usually measured in ounces. One ounce equals ¹⁄₆₄ inch (0.4 mm) in thickness, and the most commonly used thicknesses are 2 to 4 ounces, or ¹⁄₃₂ inch to ¹⁄₁₆ inch (0.8 to 1.6 mm). In my style of bookbinding, I use the simplest tool to cut leather to size: a pair of sharp scissors.

In this book, I worked with a variety of leather types including vegetable-tanned, buckskin, and

stoned-oil hides. Keep in mind that even though leather is a material with many benefits, its production, which often involves a toxic chemical process, can strongly impact the environment and natural water sources. I recommend seeking out local artisan tanners who use natural tanning methods, such as vegetable tanning or brain tanning (the process used for buckskin). Both these types of leathers are tanned without the use of toxic chemicals that are destructive to ecosystems and to the well-being of production workers. When the pages of your leather journal become filled, consider removing them and sewing in fresh ones! This way you'll get more use from the leather. Additionally, consider reusing leather from other projects or sourcing secondhand or scrap leather from upholstery and leather shops.

Many of the projects in this book feature vegetable-tanned leather in neutral peach tones as well as stoned-oil cowhide in rich earth tones. The color of unfinished vegetable-tanned leather will change quickly over time, becoming darker and developing a beautiful, shiny patina with use. Stoned-oil leather has a rich, aged look and will also darken with time and use. If you purchase your leather in a large quantity, such as by the roll or side shoulder, you will have the option to use the "live" or raw, organic-shaped edges of the leather for your projects. (*Live edge* is the term for the raw edge of a piece of leather or wood that is left as is, or unrefined.) I often position the live edge at the end of a wraparound book cover for a more rustic, natural look.

If leather is not a material you wish to work with, you can experiment with other materials in its place. Thick fabrics such as upholstery fabric, denim, raw canvas, and waxed canvas might serve as alternative cover materials and can be sourced from your own stash or your local fabric shop.

Board

Board, the hard material for the core of the cover, is essential to making a classic hardcover book. Below are a few types of board and their uses.

BINDER'S BOARD is commonly used by bookbinders. It is acid-free and comes in a range of thicknesses. I choose a $\frac{1}{16}$-inch (1.6 mm) board for most of my small to medium-sized books because it is easy to cut by hand or with a small guillotine paper cutter.

Another type that I use is acid-free **MUSEUM BOARD**. Often I cover the front and back of the board with decorative paper or cloth and leave the board edges raw so the color is exposed. Museum board ranges in thickness from $\frac{1}{32}$ inch to $\frac{1}{16}$ inch (0.8 to 1.6 mm) and is easy to cut by hand. Both binder's board and museum board can be found in an art or specialty bookbinding store.

USED BOOKS can be an abundant, inexpensive source of book board. Intercepting discarded hardcover books on the way to the dump is a great way to keep materials from going to waste. Ask your librarians or bookstore owners if they have a discard box from which you can salvage your materials. Thrift stores, yard sales, and estate sales are sources worth checking out as well. Vintage cloth-covered books are the easiest to salvage because the cloth, in most cases, will easily peel from the boards.

WOOD BOARDS are the most protective and strongest types of boards used for bookbinding. Often, the board is not covered, so the beauty of the wood grain can be appreciated. You can find boards in sheets at your local hardware store or bookbinding shop. I prefer a solid wood board that is about $\frac{3}{16}$-inch (5 mm) thick with a raw or unfinished surface. Be sure the wood you choose is a hardwood that has been dried so that it will not warp or crack after you have bound it. Always position the grain of the wood horizontally on your cover to decrease the chance of it cracking along the grain.

To cut your wood boards to size, you will need a simple handsaw. Use a wood drill to make the holes for attaching the boards to the text block. In addition to these tools, have a fine-grain sheet of sandpaper on hand to smooth the cut edges and holes.

DECONSTRUCTING A HARDCOVER

If you've sourced a used hardcover, cloth-covered book, carefully deconstruct it with the following steps:

1. Protect your work surface with a cutting board or layer of cardboard. Lay the book on your work surface. Open the front cover to expose the seam or hinge between the right edge of the front cover board and the end page.

2. Place a metal straightedge ruler along the left edge of the seam. Gently run a craft knife along the edge of the ruler (over the seam) from top to bottom. It may take a couple passes to slice through the multiple layers of paper and binding material. Use care to only slice through the material on the inside of the cover; avoid slicing into the cover and the spine itself. Once the front of the text block has completely separated from the front cover, turn to the back of the book and expose the inside of the back cover.

3. Again, position the straightedge ruler and run the craft knife along the seam between the back cover and the spine of the text block until they separate. Once you completely slice through the layers of paper, the text block should no longer be bound to the hard cover.

4. Remove the text block and set it aside.

5. To separate the cover spine from the front and back covers, place the open cover on a cutting mat, outside facing up. Position the metal ruler on the cover spine panel ¼ inch

(6 mm) from the front cover board. With a craft knife, cut the spine panel from the front cover by gently running the blade along the metal ruler. Reposition the ruler on the spine panel ¼ inch (6 mm) from the back cover board and repeat **(A)**.

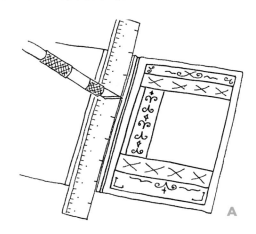

A

6. Turn one of the cover boards over so the back side is facing up. Gently peel the liner paper from the inside of the board. Once the paper is removed, peel the wraparound edges of cloth from the board. Once all four edges of cloth are peeled off, turn the board around and remove the cloth from the outside of the cover. Repeat for the remaining cover board.

7. Using a guillotine paper cutter or a craft knife with a metal ruler, trim your boards to size according to the project instructions. Once trimmed, they are ready for your next project!

Cloth

Try experimenting with cloth as a book cover. It can be a simple, effective way to bring texture and beauty to your hand-bound book.

THICK CLOTH, such as heavyweight raw canvas, waxed canvas, denim, felted wool, and upholstery cloth, is often rigid and durable enough to serve as a wraparound book cover. Highlight the beauty of antique **HAND-EMBROIDERED LINEN CLOTH** by adhering it to book boards or glue basic **COTTON SHEET CLOTH** to boards and decorate with fabric paints and markers. Regardless of what type of cloth you choose to use, it is one material that can be found in abundance at your local fabric shop or can be upcycled from thrift and secondhand stores.

Closures

In this book, I chose to keep the closures simple by experimenting with cordage and leather ties and finding ways to use up smaller pieces of scrap leather rather than letting them go to waste.

LINEN BOOKBINDING THREAD can be twined or braided together to create a strong cord for securing covers of your book. You will make a **LEATHER BUTTON** in two projects (pages 38 and 101). Other projects call for a simple **LEATHER TIE** or **CORD** to wrap around the cover and protect the contents of the book.

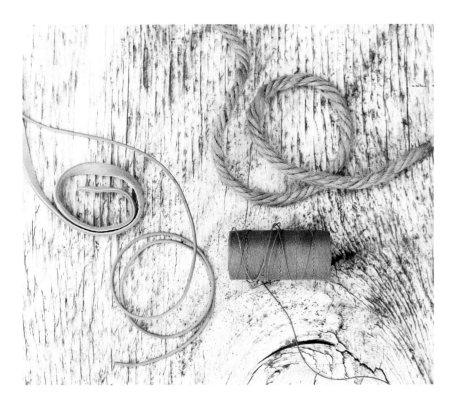

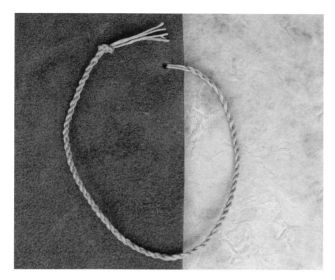

TOOLS AND SUPPLIES

Below you'll find a selection of basic tools you'll almost always need, along with short lists of additional needed items.

Bone Folder

A bookbinding essential that is traditionally made of polished bone, it is used to press along the spine (the fold part) of a signature to create an even, crisp fold line. Bone folders are available in many sizes and shapes.

Bookbinding Thread (Binder's Thread)

As in any sewing project, thread holds it all together. High-quality archival bookbinding thread is made from linen, an extremely strong, durable fiber derived from the flax plant. Bookbinding thread is available in a variety of thicknesses, or plies: 18/3 or 12/3 ply is adequate for general bookbinding and all the projects featured here. The higher the first number, the thinner the thread. The second number refers to the number of strands used to make the thread.

Linen bookbinding thread is available waxed or unwaxed. If you choose unwaxed thread, you will want to coat it yourself by running it over a block of natural beeswax (page 9). You may also consider other nonelastic threads such as buttonhole thread, thin hemp thread, metallic thread, and upholstery thread.

Binding Post

One way to bind a book without sewing is to use a binding screw post—a cylindrical screw-type

ADDITIONAL MATERIALS NEEDED

* India ink

* Fabric markers

* Paint markers

* Acrylic paint

* Scrap wood

* Variety of vegetables, herbs, and tea

* Variety of wool darning thread and embroidery thread

* Hair elastic

* Ribbon

* Shoe box

* Thumbtacks

* Wooden dowel

connector that goes through the covers and text block. Binding posts come in a variety of lengths and widths and are made of different metal compositions. The width and length are the most important aspects to consider when purchasing one. You will want the post to be sized specifically as stated in the project directions. You can find binding posts at bookbinding shops as well as in the hardware section in leather stores.

Glue

Polyvinyl acetate (PVA) glue is a common paper glue that will dry quickly and will be clear. It is water-based, so it is easily cleaned up with warm, soapy water. Another traditional binding glue is all-natural wheat paste, which often comes as a powder that you hydrate and mix at home. Both are available from most art stores and specialty bookbinding shops.

Glue Brush

To spread glue onto the materials, use a small, round-tipped glue brush, or you can also get by with an inexpensive flat-head paintbrush. Immediately after use, be sure to rinse the brush with warm, soapy water and then dry the bristles with a cotton cloth or hang it, brush-side down, to air dry.

Awl

An awl is used for punching holes in paper as well as in cover boards. Traditionally, an awl is made from a thin tapered metal shaft with a wooden handle. A $\frac{3}{16}$-inch (5 mm) metal shaft is ideal for punching paper. You might want to try a slightly wider-shafted awl for punching through cover board so the shaft does not bend as it penetrates the harder material. You may also use a large safety pin, upholstery needle, T-pin, or a thin sharp nail.

Bookbinding Needle

Use a small-eyed, blunt bookbinding needle to sew your punched signatures together. The needle's point is blunt so it won't inadvertently pierce or scratch the page—or you. Thin, strong needles are ideal for sewing through the small holes in the signatures and often can be found at specialty bookbinding shops. If you are unable to access a bookbinding needle, use a needle that has as little tapering from eye to point as possible.

Beeswax

Beeswax is used to coat raw binder's thread. It protects thread from friction, allows it to glide more freely through the holes, keeps knots from forming in the thread line, and creates knots that are less likely to slip. (See page 16 for more information.)

Pencil

Use a simple No. 2 pencil for making marks. Be sure to have a sharpener on hand.

Craft Knife

A craft knife can be used for cutting lightweight material such as book board. It consists of a metal handle with a replaceable sharp triangular blade.

Metal Ruler

A ruler is extremely useful for measuring and for drawing straight lines. I switch between an 18-inch (45.7 cm) metal-edge ruler with a no-slip cork backing for large measurements and a 6-inch (15.2 cm) metal ruler for smaller ones.

Scissors

A sharp pair of scissors is indispensable. A small pair is best for trimming the threads in hard-to-reach places, while a large pair is effective for general use and for rounding signatures or cutting paper, thread, lightweight board, cloth, and leather.

Paper Cutter

A couple of options are available: a guillotine (swinging-arm cutter) has a gridded baseboard with a bladed arm that swings down to chop the paper. The other variant is a rotary trimmer with a flat bed, which has a sliding shuttle with a rotating circular blade that slices paper. I exclusively use a guillotine to cut paper and thin boards. I have a 16-inch (40.6 cm) guillotine cutter for small papers and a 25-inch (63.5 cm) cutter for large-format papers.

Hole Punch

Hole punches are used for punching neat, clean holes through thicker materials such as leather and binder's board. They come in a variety of styles, such as rotary, hollow punch, or screw punch and offer a wide range of hole sizes. Most often, I reach for my handheld rotary punch, as it is the most versatile and the hole size adjusts with a simple rotation of the wheel. When sewing pockets onto leather covers, I use the 1/16-inch (2 mm) setting that is available on my small rotary punch. I turn to my 3/16-inch (5 mm) punch to make cover holes along the spine and for attaching ties and buttons.

Rubber Bands and Binder Clips

These are used for holding sheets or stacks of paper together and keeping signatures in order. A variety of sizes will be needed to accommodate the variable thickness of stacks.

Cutting Mat

A self-healing cutting mat protects your work surface and provides a surface for cutting with a craft or utility knife. Eco-friendly alternatives include a sheet of cardboard or an old wooden tabletop that can handle wear and tear.

Phone Book or Punching Cradle

A phone book or punching cradle is handy to have for punching holes in signatures. It nests the fold (or spine) of the signature to keep the sheets of paper neatly together, and it provides protection so you're not damaging your work surface—or your hands— each time you punch your awl through. (See page 15 for more on punching holes in signatures.)

Corner Rounder

This optional tool is used to punch the corners of pages to create a rounded edge. It can add a nice, professional touch to a handmade book. Small, hand-held rounders are available, but if you intend to cut more than a couple of sheets at a time or cut through binder's board, consider investing in a heavy-duty tabletop rounder. Although they're more expensive, their performance is worth it.

ADDITIONAL TOOLS NEEDED

* Electric drill with wood and diamond drill bits
* Dust mask
* Safety glasses
* Handsaw (to cut wood covers)
* Heavy object (such as a book or weight) or a book press

* Small water tub, approximately 20 × 15 inches (7.8 × 5.9 cm)
* Sandpaper
* Embroidery needles
* Saucepan
* Baking dish
* Carpenter's hammer
* Masking tape

* Dressmaker's pins
* Mesh strainer
* Wax paper
* Paper bag
* Towels
* Rubber mallet
* Leather stamping tools
* Sponge

BASIC BOOKBINDING TOOLKIT

1 Scissors

2 Awl, ³⁄₁₆-inch (5 mm) metal shaft

3 Large rotary hole punch for leather and board

4 Binder's thread

5 Glue brush

6 6-inch (15 cm) metal ruler

7 Pencil

8 Beeswax

9 Bookbinder's needle

10 Small rotary hole punch for leather and paper

11 Bone folder

NOT PICTURED: *18-inch metal ruler, glue, paper cutter, phonebook*

THE ANATOMY OF A BOOK

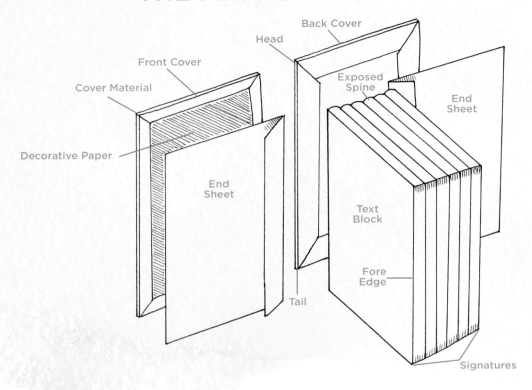

Back Cover

Head

Front Cover

Cover Material

Exposed Spine

End Sheet

Decorative Paper

End Sheet

Text Block

Fore Edge

Tail

Signatures

BASIC TECHNIQUES

Throughout the book, I will refer you to this section for detailed instructions on basic stitching patterns and techniques.

Making a Text Block

The text block is the heart of the book. It is often made up of writing paper or handmade paper that has been folded into signatures. The front and back signatures of the block are often wrapped with decorative end pages. There is a general sequence of steps to follow when making a text block, though with very simple books some steps may be omitted. Detailed instructions will be provided in each project.

Folding Signatures

The first thing to do is to decide whether you will be folding with or against the grain of the paper. In traditional book arts, binders are taught to fold with the grain of the paper—that is, with the grain running parallel to the spine of the signature. This has several benefits: easier folding, pages that turn more readily, and less likelihood of the text block warping and compromising the strength of the binding. By all means, if you wish to go with the grain, rest assured it is a time-proven method with obvious benefits.

On the other hand, I offer this perspective: In our time of diminishing natural resources, such as forests and clean water, I believe it vitally important to

DETERMINING THE GRAIN OF YOUR PAPER

The grain of the paper refers to the direction in which the fibers in the paper run. By folding with the grain you will break fewer of the fibers with the fold. Doing so will help your text block maintain its structural integrity. To fold against the grain could potentially weaken the paper and result in warping of the text block in some types of bindings, especially in a hardbound book. Fortunately, since the projects in this book use a simple folk-style binding, they allow a lot of flexibility when it comes to grain. If you wish to take a purer approach, I encourage you go online to research "paper grain direction," as there is much more information available online than can be covered in the limited space in this book.

You can determine grain direction by a couple of very simple means. One of the easiest is to check the dimensions of the paper given on the package. The grain direction is usually listed as the last dimension of the paper's sheet size. For example, an 8½ × 11–inch sheet of paper would be grain long, meaning that the fibers are running in the 11-inch direction. Sometimes the grain direction is specified in boldface type on the package—8½ × **11** inches would mean that the paper is grain long, whereas **8½** × 11 inches would mean that it's grain short.

Another way to find the grain is to conduct a fold test with a sheet of paper. First, place a sheet of paper on a table. Then fold the paper lengthwise without making a crease. The paper will form a smooth arch near where the fold would be. With your other hand, test the bounce, or "give," of the arch. Ask yourself, *How easily does it want to fold?* Fold the paper without creasing in the other direction, and test that arch as well. Compare the difference between the two directions. The grain is likely running in the same direction as the fold that has the least resistance.

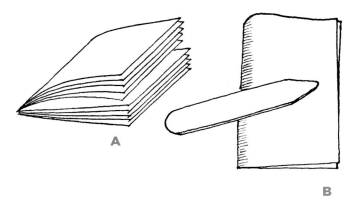

upcycle and reuse as often as possible, especially in the realm of paper products. When I sourced paper for the projects in this book, I sought out recycled paper as well as paper left over from other projects. I had an abundance of paper to use but not always in an adequate quantity for folding with the grain, which typically requires more paper. I chose the less perfect, though more eco-conscious path and often folded my signatures against the grain. However you choose to fold, do keep it consistent: If you fold against the grain for one signature, be sure to do it for all of the signatures in the book.

1. To fold your paper into a signature, gather the number of sheets of paper as detailed in the instructions (usually 4 to 8 sheets) and group them into a stack.

2. Align the stack by gently tapping (or jogging) the bottom and one side edge on your work surface.

3. Lay the stack on your table and firmly press one side of the paper to the table while you fold the other over to align the pressed edges **(A)**.

4. Secure the loose edges of the papers with one hand. With the bone folder in your other hand, gently crease the fold, beginning halfway down the signature and sliding to one end of the paper's fold. To finish, place the bone folder in the center of the fold and complete the fold in the other direction **(B)**.

Making a Template

Most projects will require you to make a template for punching the sewing stations, holes through which the needle and thread can pass to bind the signatures together, or making a specific part of the book. In each of the projects, I've included a template that you can simply copy onto cardstock. Some templates will need to be enlarged to reach 100 percent with a photocopier or scanner first (there is a note with these templates that indicates the percentage to enlarge). There are a couple of ways of making templates—the best choice depends on your available resources.

METHOD 1: PHOTOCOPYING

This method may be used for all templates: ones that need to be enlarged and ones that are printed to size in this book. Use your home computer and scanner, or visit your local copy shop and use a photocopier. Place the page with the template facedown on the scanner flatbed. Enlarge the image (if necessary) and then scan in grayscale. Print the template file onto a sheet of white cardstock. Cut the template from the cardstock and punch any holes indicated with an awl.

This method is used only for templates that are printed to size in this book. Place a sheet of translucent tracing paper over the template in the book and trace the lines with a pencil. Layer the tracing paper over a sheet of carbon paper and place both on top of the cardstock. Use a pencil to retrace the template lines and any dots, indicating where holes are to be punched. The carbon paper will transfer the lines onto the cardstock. Take care to hold the papers in place while tracing so the copy of the template remains true to size. Then set the tracing and carbon papers aside. Cut the template from the cardstock and use an awl to punch any holes indicated on the template. You may need to number the holes and label the orientation (top/bottom) of the template with an arrow if the binding is complex. (Note that some of the more complex templates are already numbered for you to help keep track of the sewing stations.)

Punching the Sewing Stations

After you have folded the signatures, the next step in making a text block is punching sewing stations into the signatures. Many of the projects provide detailed punching templates that will guide you in the proper placement of each sewing station. Templates are integral in creating consistently punched signatures in a time-efficient manner.

1. Make the template with the cardstock using one of the methods described in the previous section.

2. Open the first signature of the text block, and place it in the fold of an open phone book or inside a punching cradle if you have one. Nest the open template inside the signature (in the matching top/bottom orientation) and gently punch the sewing stations with an awl **(A)**.

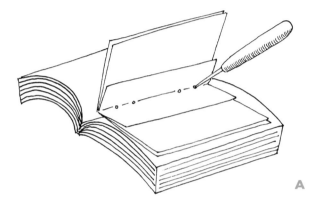

A

Tip: Make the holes as small and neat as possible by using a thin and narrowly tapered awl—a ³⁄₁₆-inch (5 mm) metal shaft is ideal. This is especially important in exposed spine bindings where the holes will remain visible.

3. Remove that signature and replace it with an unpunched one. Continue to punch the signatures according to the project instructions, following the template. After punching the holes, stack the signatures in their proper order. You may also temporarily bind the signatures with a binder clip or rubber band to keep them in place until you are ready to sew them together.

Preparing the Cover

Cover preparation varies according to the material used. Each project will provide instructions or a template for drilling or punching the cover holes. In general, mark the holes for attaching the cover to the text block with a pencil according to the template and punch them with an awl or hole punch. Some materials (such as wood and stone) may require a drill and drill bit. In either case, be sure to punch or drill the holes by starting on the outside of the cover. This will ensure that the rough side of the puncture will be hidden on the inside of the cover.

Preparing the Binder's Thread

Linen bookbinder's thread is available waxed or unwaxed. The waxed thread is ready to use, but the unwaxed thread will need to be coated with beeswax, which you can do yourself. The wax helps protect the thread from fraying, keeps it from sliding out of the needle, locks the stitches, and allows it to slide more readily through the sewing stations. Beeswax also leaves behind a pleasing, delicate honey aroma.

1. To wax the thread, run it from end to end two or three times over a block of solid (room-temperature) beeswax **(A)**.

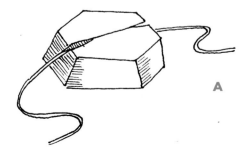

A

2. To thread the needle, run one end of the waxed thread through the needle's eye. Do not fasten the thread by tying a knot; leave a loose tail 2 to 3 inches (5 to 7.5 cm) long instead. Pinch the thread together around the eye, allowing the beeswax to help lock the thread in place on the needle.

The projects in this book are bound with a single-threaded needle. *Single-threaded* means that you put the end of the thread through the needle's eye, just far enough to keep it from slipping out—perhaps a few inches **(A)**. The stitches will then be made with just one thread this way.

A

Stitching

The general stitching pattern for books with multiple signatures begins with a similar series of knots to link the heads and tails of the signatures together. The signatures that make up the text blocks are joined with thread in two ways: (1) the thread travels in and out of the holes in a signature to bind the pages of the signature to each other and (2) the thread travels through the stations of signatures adjacent to the signature you are working on to link it to the text block. The joining could be at the station at the top and bottom of the signature, or it could be at more stations than just the first and last.

There are many stitches that can accomplish the joining, as will be described later. The following demonstration gives a general idea of how a group of signatures is bound together. Before you start, place the signatures in front of you, aligned with the folded edges facing you. Many projects will ask you to pull signatures from the bottom of the stack as you sew them into the text block. Because some signatures are punched uniquely to create a design in the stitching, this will ensure the signatures stay in order and align with the holes of the cover and the overall stitching design.

1. To begin, take the first signature and guide the needle and thread into the first sewing station on your right, working from the outside of the signature to the center fold. Leave a tail of thread of the length recommended in the project on the outside of the first station. (The tail will be used later.) Continue sewing along the spine of the signature as directed for the particular project, exiting at the leftmost station to the outside of the signature.

2. Once the needle has exited the last station, place the next signature on top of the first and make a direct link, inserting the needle into the nearest sewing station of the second signature. Continue sewing down the spine of the second signature and link the signature to the first one as directed for that particular project. You will now be traveling from left to right in sewing, opposite to signature 1.

3. Once the needle has exited out the last station (far right), you will need to link to the tail thread of the first signature with a square knot (page 28). Allow the tail thread to hang in the opposite direction, away from the recently added signature.

4. Place the third signature on top of the second and draw the needle and thread directly into the nearest station of signature 3 **(A)**. Continue sewing down the spine of the third signature according to project instructions.

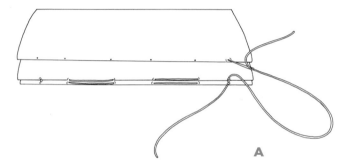

A

5. Once the needle has exited the last station of signature 3, link to the previous signature with a true kettle stitch **(B)**. See page 23 for instructions for the true kettle stitch.

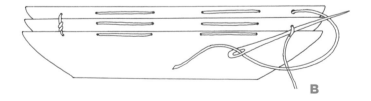

B

6. From here on out, use a true kettle stitch to link at each end of each signature.

7. Finish the binding by linking to the previous signature with a true kettle stitch.

8. Leave a loose tail of thread at the end. This will be used later to attach the covers.

RUNNING STITCH

This simple stitch is a widely used technique implemented in most of the projects throughout this book. It can be applied to a variety of book structures, such as one with an exposed spine or a book with a leather or wraparound cover. In its simplest form, it consists of a simple straight stitch that weaves down the spine of a signature **(A)**.

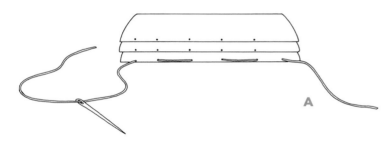

In my projects you'll find the running stitch is often combined with other stitches to make a strong and attractive binding. Sometimes, the spine stitching of multiple signatures may be gathered or woven together in the last signature or after stitching is complete to strengthen the binding and add ornamentation (see Gathering Stitch, page 24, and Weaving Stitch, page 50). Tapes (rectangular tabs of paper, ribbon, or cloth) can be sized to fit between the sewing stations on the exterior of the spine and sewn over with the running stitches **(B)** to further strengthen and add an ornamental quality to the binding (see Garland of Gratitude on page 52).

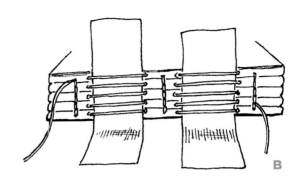

PAMPHLET STITCH

This basic binding structure is a quick and simple method of binding a small book with few pages. It usually consists of one signature, but may also be applied to multiple signatures within a case, the separately created book cover, to accommodate a book of greater thickness. The stitching pattern can also be repeated within one signature to double the number of exposed threads and allow for the stitching to be woven on for decorative and strengthening purposes (see The Visionary, page 79).

1. Place the signature with the spine facing you. To make a basic pamphlet stitch, place the tip of the threaded needle in through the outside of the center sewing station and draw the thread into the center of the signature, leaving a 3-inch (7.6 cm) tail on the outside of the spine.

2. Guide the needle into the leftmost sewing station and pull the thread to the outside of the spine **(A)**.

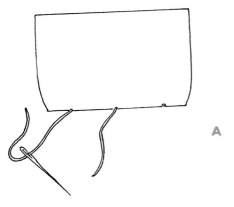

A

3. Draw the needle into the rightmost sewing station, skipping over the center station entirely, and pull the thread to the inside of the spine **(B)**.

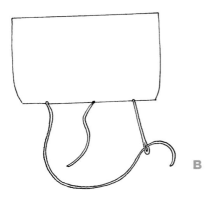

B

4. Complete the stitch by guiding the needle through the center station from the inside of the signature to the outside of the spine, **(C)**. Tighten all threads. Remove the needle and bind the loose thread ends with a square knot (page 28).

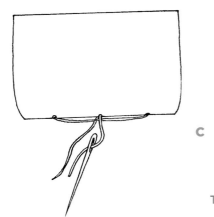

C

If you prefer to hide your finishing knot on the inside of the pamphlet, the binding can also begin inside the signature, thus ending with the binding knot inside and hidden from view (see The Visionary, page 79).

LONG STITCH

This medieval binding technique is a simple and effective way to attach the text block directly to a leather or cloth cover at the same time the signatures are joined into a text block. The stitching pattern involves a long stitch that weaves in and out of the sewing stations. It is similar to the running stitch (page 18), but it does not use true kettle stitches to link the signatures together at the ends. Instead, the long stitch links directly (page 143) from one signature to the next. Because true kettle stitches are not used, it is important that each signature is firmly attached to the cover's spine and that there is no slack in the thread. The long-stitch pattern can be modified to allow for decorative stitches, such as French stitches (page 23) or weaving along the outside of the spine (see The Mystic, page 90, and Weaver of Dreams, page 36).

Before you start, you will need to prepare the cover and punch the sewing stations on what will become the spine of the book. Arrange the cover so it is oriented vertically with the fore edge of the cover facing you and the back side facing up. Stack the text block signatures nearby with their spines facing you.

Here is a general stitching pattern for the long stitch **(A)**:

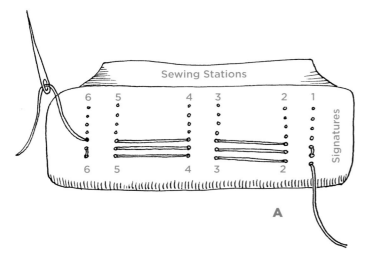

A

1. Signature 1: Lift the front edge of the cover and enter the threaded needle into the rightmost station (sewing station 1) of row 1 on the cover's spine. Pull a signature from the bottom of the pile and place it inside the cover so the holes in the spine align with the stations in row. Draw the thread into the interior of the signature. Leave a tail length according to project instructions on the outside of the cover. Continue sewing with a series of running stitches (page 18) through both layers (signature spine and cover spine) until you arrive at the outside of the cover on the leftmost station (station 6, in this case). Make sure to pull the thread taut at the completion of every stitch so the binding is strong and there is no slack in the thread.

2. Signature 2: Enter into the closest hole in row 2 on the outside of the cover (in this case station 6). Pull a signature from the bottom of the stack and align it with the row of stations above the sewn signature. Draw the needle into the nearest station of the signature and pull the thread taut. Bring the needle back to the outside of the signature through the next sewing station. Stitch down the signature, alternating between bringing the needle to the inside of the spine and then back outside the spine as you move along the sewing stations.

3. Continue with the long-stitch pattern to bind the remaining signatures in the same way.

4. After the last signature is attached, weave the threaded needle in and out of the top stations near the head of the spine to fill in the threadless gaps between the end stations. Once all gaps are filled, enter into the nearest signature and tie off (see page 27). Trim the thread ends to ¼ inch (6 mm).

5. Thread the remaining tail of thread at station 1, row 1 onto the needle and repeat step 4 at the tail of the spine.

CHAIN STITCH

This linking stitch creates a minimal, clean pattern on an exposed spine. There are several methods used to begin this stitching pattern. I've chosen one that forms a loop in the first signature that will be tightened later.

1. Begin by entering the rightmost sewing station (1) of your first signature from the outside of the spine. Draw the thread to the inside of the signature, leaving a 6- to 12-inch (15.2 to 30.5 cm) tail on the outside.

2. Draw the thread through sewing station 2 to the outside of the signature **(A)**. Reenter sewing station 2 and pull the thread until a small loop forms on the outside of the signature.

3. Guide the needle into station 3 from the inside, taking care not to pull the loop out of the previous station.

4. Pull the next signature from the bottom of the text block and place it on top of your first signature, checking that the sewing stations are aligned. Direct-link into the next signature at the nearest station and pull the thread semi-taut **(B)**.

5. Guide the needle out of the next sewing station in signature 2 (in this case station 2) and through the loop of thread on the previous signature **(C)**.

6. Carefully pull the thread at the beginning of the binding taut so the loop of thread cinches closed. Return the needle back into the station it just came out of and pull the thread taut **(D)**.

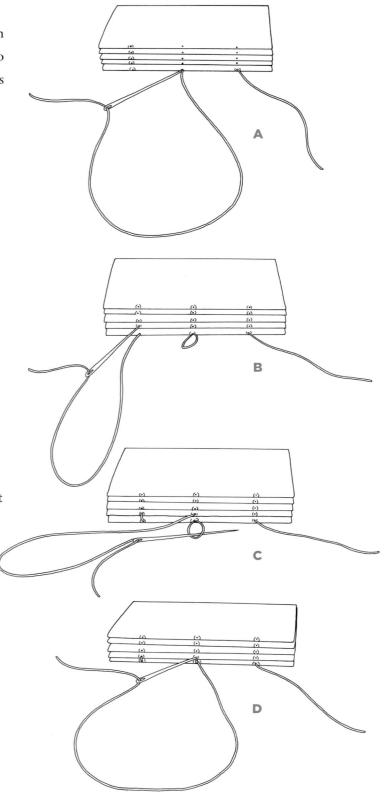

A

B

C

D

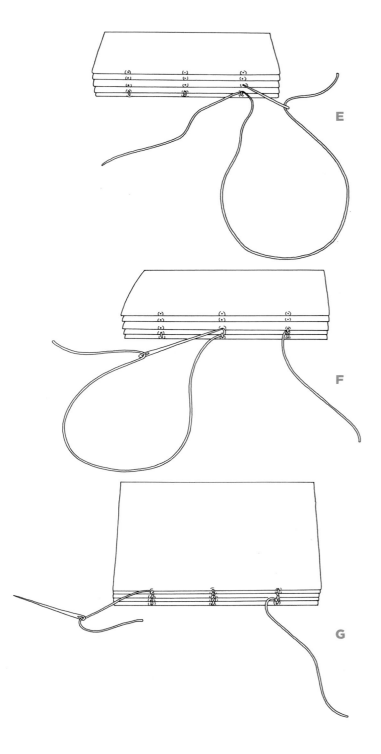

7. Continue to the next sewing station. Starting from the inside of the second signature, draw the thread to the outside of the rightmost station. Link to the previous signature using a square knot (page 28).

8. Add a new signature on top of the sewn one and direct link into the rightmost station (station 1) **(E)**.

9. Link the center station to the previous one with a chain stitch by wrapping the thread once around the link between the previous two signatures; then return the needle into the center station of the third signature **(F)**.

10. Link the leftmost station to the previous signature's leftmost station with a true kettle stitch (page 23).

11. Continue adding signatures by linking the center station to the previous one with a chain stitch around the link between the previous two signatures **(G)**. For each new signature, link the bottom station to the nearest sewing station of the previous signature using a true kettle stitch (page 23). Link the top stations together in the same way. Leave the tails long to use for attaching the covers (page 24).

TRUE KETTLE STITCH

Of all the stitches, this is the one that, when executed correctly, brings the most structure to your bindings. The true kettle stitch is used to link the heads of signatures to each other and tails of the signatures to each other. To do this, guide the needle under the stitch that links the previous signatures, starting from the inside of the spine and pulling the needle toward the outside left or right of the spine (depending on which end of the signatures you are at). Continue to pull the thread until there is a small loop remaining. Guide the needle through the loop and tighten the stitch, pulling toward the most recent signature so the needle will easily point into the next signature **(A)**.

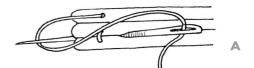

A

FRENCH STITCH

This Old World stitch is an elegant way of linking threads along an exposed spine (see Reverence, page 132).

1. Begin with a series of running stitches along the spine of the first signature.

2. Add the second signature and draw the needle directly into the adjacent hole in the second signature to link.

3. Continue sewing the signature with a running stitch that wraps once (or twice for a double French stitch) around the previous signature's running stitch **(A)**.

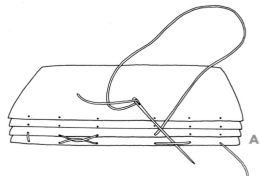

A

4. Before linking the current signature with a true kettle stitch (page 23), always make sure the thread is pulled taut throughout the sewing stations; otherwise, your signature might be sewn too loosely and will compromise the strength of the overall binding.

5. In the following signatures you add, continue to wrap around the closest leg of the previous signature's thread. The French pattern will begin to emerge as you add signatures to the sewn spine **(B)**.

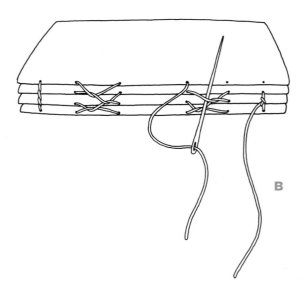

B

GATHERING STITCH

A gathering stitch may be used to strengthen a running-stitch binding by linking multiple signatures together. This stitch is often made while stitching the final signature. The gathering stitch is made on the spine stitches of the text block. (See Morning Ritual, page 32.)

1. Pull the thread to the outside of the signature at the station designated in the project. Guide the needle beneath the running or long stitches of the previous signatures **(A)** and pull the thread back toward the final signature.

2. Loop into the working thread near the current sewing station and pull the thread tight until all the running or long stitch threads gather and a knot is formed **(B)**. Be sure to center the knot between the sewing stations.

3. Reinforce the stitch by repeating this knot around all threads. Pull tight and enter into the next sewing station **(C)**.

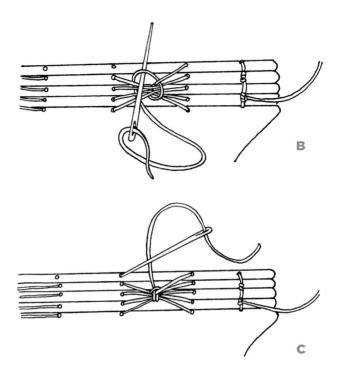

B

C

Attaching the Covers and Hiking Down the Spine

Often, though not always, a book's cover is attached during the sewing of the text block. For an exposed-spine binding, I've found it easier to attach the heads and tails of the covers after the spine is sewn. To accommodate, I always leave 10 to 12 inches (25.4 to 30.5 cm) of loose thread at the beginning and end of the binding and add this to the thread length recommended in the individual projects. The method shown here will work for books with an odd number of signatures.

1. If the cover boards aren't already in place after the final signature is sewn to the text block, set the boards in place. Align the book so the spine is facing you.

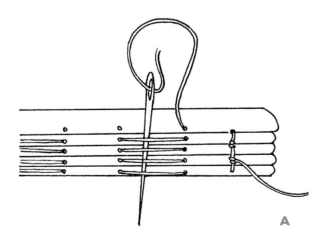

A

If your thread does not already have a needle attached, thread a needle with the loose end of thread hanging from the last signature sewn. Guide the needle around the outside of the spine edge of the front cover board and into the hole on the top of the cover board **(A)**.

3. Again, guide the thread toward the outside of the cover and into the same hole **(C)**.

4. Draw the needle down and around the outside of the cover's edge and pull the thread taut **(D)**.

5. Draw the needle under the linking stitch between the previous signatures **(E)** and pull the thread taut.

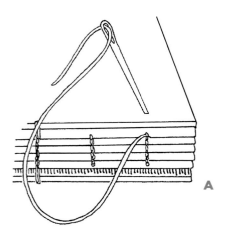

A

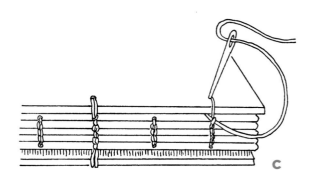

C

2. Draw the needle down through the cover and around to the outside of the cover's spine edge and pull the thread taut. Loop the needle around the linking stitch between the two previous signatures **(B)** and pull the thread taut.

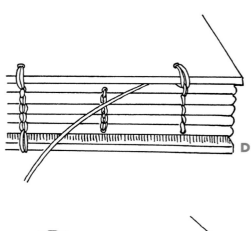

D

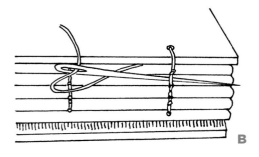

B

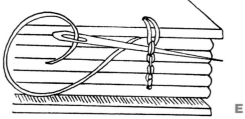

E

6. Continue to loop the needle and thread around the linking stitches across the spine by using a simple technique I call "hiking." Hiking the thread down the first sewing station of all the signatures and the last sewing station of all the signatures reinforces the structure of the exposed binding and allows the thread to effectively travel from the front cover to the back cover, or vice-versa. Draw the needle to the inside of the next linking stitch and then pass it under the stitch in between the signatures and toward the edge of the spine **(F)**. Pull the thread taut. Continue hiking down the top of the spine, linking stitches by wrapping the thread once around each of the linking stitches **(G)** and pulling the thread taut each time until you reach the bottom signature **(H)**.

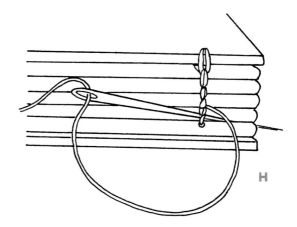

H

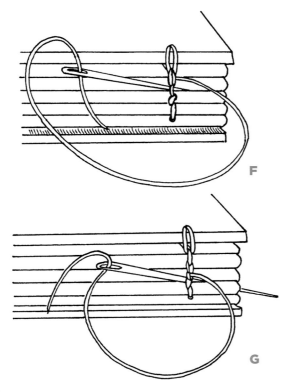

F

G

7. Turn the text block over so the back cover is facing up. If the back cover is not yet in place, position it on the text block so its top and bottom holes align with the top and bottom holes of the sewing stations. Attach the hole of the back cover using the same double-loop method as you used for the front cover. Do not travel back up the spine with the thread. Instead, guide the needle into the nearest hole of the bottom signature and tie the thread off inside (see Tying Off the Binding, page 27). Remove the needle from the end of the thread.

8. Thread the needle onto the remaining tail at the other end of the spine. Repeat the method described in steps 1–7 to attach the cover and hike down the spine at this end of the book.

Tying Off the Binding

After you've completed sewing the signatures and the covers are attached (either one side or both), you'll need to tie off the binding to secure it. If your needle is not threaded, pick up the tail at either end of the text block.

1. Enter into the nearest signature **(A)** and pull the thread taut on the inside of the signature **(B)**.

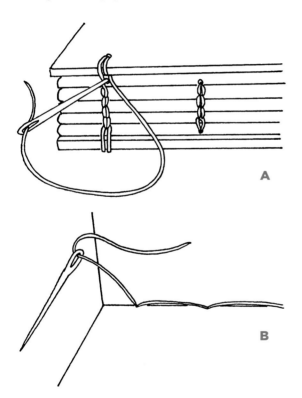

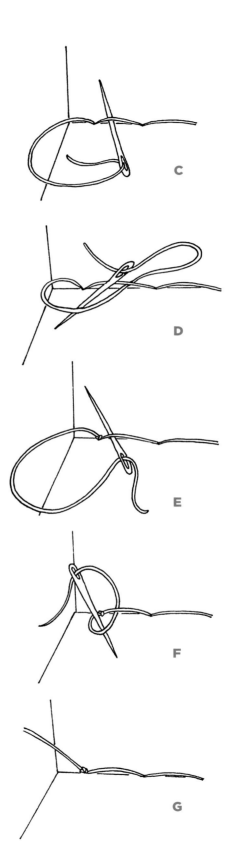

2. Guide the needle underneath the signature thread between the nearest sewing stations and make a true kettle stitch **(C, D)** (page 23). Repeat the stitch again **(E, F)**, and tighten to make a knot **(G)**; then trim the thread to ¼ inch (6 mm).

Other Knots, Stitches, and Techniques

Throughout the book, I will refer to the following knots and stitches, which are best instructed through illustration.

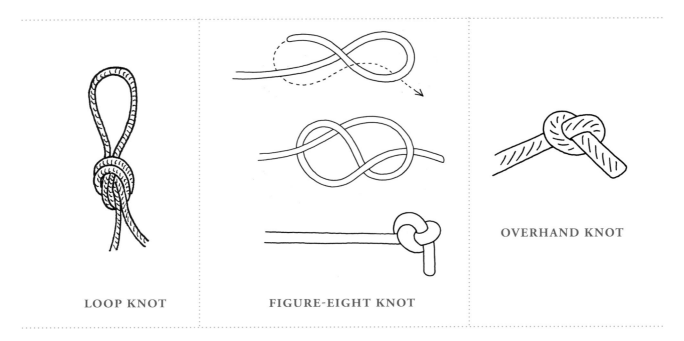

LOOP KNOT

FIGURE-EIGHT KNOT

OVERHAND KNOT

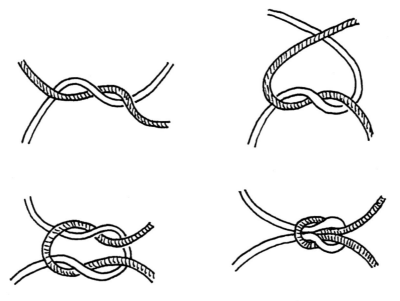

SQUARE KNOT

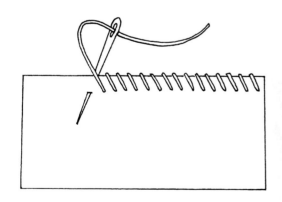

WHIP KNOT

OVERHAND STITCH (ALSO CALLED WHIPSTITCH OR OVERCAST STITCH)

ANCHORING THREAD

When you're adding decorative stitching to a book that has already been bound, or adding new thread because you ran out as you were sewing, the first thing that you need to do is to anchor the new thread.

This is very similar to tying off a binding (page 27), but instead of cutting the thread, you will attach a new length of thread to the inside of a signature using a square knot and then begin stitching according project instructions.

1. Thread the needle with a new length of thread.

2. Open the signature according to the project instructions.

3. Attach the loose end of the thread to the running stitch on the inside of the signature using a square knot (page 28). Leave a ½-inch (1.3 cm) tail. Be sure to position the knot near the hole into which you will be entering the needle.

4. Enter the needle into the nearest station. Draw it to the outside of the cover or to the other side of the material to begin your binding or decorative stitching.

JOURNALS
for EVERYDAY
PRACTICE

MORNING RITUAL

QUIETLY BEGIN YOUR DAY AND CENTER YOUR THOUGHTS WITH
A WARM CUP OF TEA AND THESE TEA-STEEPED PAGES.

Finished Dimensions

5 × 7 × 1 inches (12.7 × 17.8 × 2.5 cm)

Binding Techniques

Long-stitch variation
(page 19)

Gathering stitch (page 24)

What You Need

Basic Bookbinding Toolkit (page 11)

Bookbinding thread, 95 inches (241.3 cm)

2 binder's boards, 5¼ × 7⅛ inches
(13.3 × 18.1 cm)

18 sheets of 90 lb. (190 gsm) hot-pressed
watercolor paper, 10 × 7 inches (25.4 × 17.8 cm)

Cardstock for template

2 embroidered linen napkins, 7 × 8½ inches
(17.8 × 21.6 cm)

1 ounce (28 g) dried black tea leaves

4 cups (1 liter) water

1-quart (1 liter) saucepan

Mesh strainer

Baking pan, 9 × 12 inches (22.9 × 30.5 cm)

4 to 6 large bath towels

Wax paper

Heavy object or book press

Note: Choose old or dark-colored towels
so it won't matter if they are stained.

DYE THE LINENS AND PAPER

1. Place the tea leaves and water in a saucepan. Bring to a boil and allow the tea to simmer for 20 minutes. While the water is hot, carefully strain the tea into the baking pan using a mesh strainer.

2. Submerge the linen napkins in the hot tea and steep until the tea cools to room temperature, about 20 minutes. Squeeze any extra water from the linens and spread them flat over a bath towel to dry.

3. Dip both sides of each sheet of watercolor paper into the tea. Let the excess tea drip back into the baking pan before laying the paper on the bath towels. Allow the paper to dry thoroughly in a well-ventilated area.

MAKE THE COVERS

4. Place a piece of wax paper to protect your work surface. Apply a thin layer of glue to one of the binder's boards. Center the board, glue-side down, onto the back of one of the linen napkins. Turn the board over and use a bone folder to smooth the napkin's surface. With the board facing up again, measure ⅛ inch (3 mm) out from each corner of the cover board and mark with a pencil. Position a ruler diagonally across each mark and draw a line **(A)**. With scissors, cut off the corners of the fabric along the pencil marks. This will reduce the bulk of fabric at the corners.

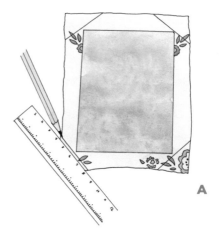

A

5. To secure the cloth edges to the back of the board, use a brush to apply a thin layer of glue to the entire bottom edge of the cloth. Fold the glued edge of the cloth up to meet the backside of the board. Use a bone folder to smooth the edge, pressing the cloth onto the board. Repeat for the top edge, then for the side edges.

6. Repeat steps 4 and 5 for the remaining board.

MAKE THE TEXT BLOCK

7. Group the sheets of watercolor paper into pairs. Fold each pair in half to make a signature measuring 5 × 7 inches (12.7 × 17.8 cm). Stack the folded signatures into a text block.

PUNCH HOLES IN THE SIGNATURES

8. Create a punch guide from Template 1 on the cardstock. Nestle the punch guide into the center of a signature and punch holes at the marks with an awl. Repeat for all the signatures.

Template 1: Signature Punch Guide, 3 × 7 inches (7.6 × 17.8 cm). Enlarge template 200%.

PUNCH HOLES IN THE COVERS

9. Fold the signature punch guide and align it with the spine edge of the cover board. Center the guide between the top and bottom edges of the cover. With a pencil, mark only the topmost and bottom-most sewing stations onto the cover ¼ inch (6 mm) from the spine edge **(B)**. Repeat for the back cover.

10. Using an awl, punch the marked holes on both covers, working from the fabric side in. You will have a total of four holes, two on each cover.

ASSEMBLE THE BOOK

11. Prepare the text block for binding by assembling all the signatures with their folds facing one way. Make certain that all the pages are in order. Orient the text block front-side up with the spine facing you.

12. Gently pull the bottom signature from the unbound text block. Thread the needle with the thread. Enter into sewing station 1 from the outside of the signature and pull the thread to the inside of the signature. Leave 8 inches (20.3 cm) of loose thread on the outside to attach the covers later. Continue sewing signature 1 using the running stitch (page 18).

13. Sew the remaining signatures in the text block, using the running stitch. Link the top and bottom sewing station of each signature to the previous one with a true kettle stitch (page 23). On the ninth and final signature, exit from station 2.

14. Make a gathering stitch using the threads from all the previous signatures (page 24). From there, continue into sewing station 3.

15. Complete the binding with a true kettle stitch at the final station **(C)**. Place the text block within the covers.

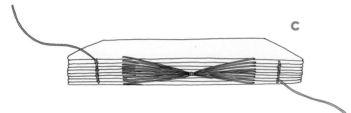

16. Use the thread tails to attach the cover (see Attaching the Covers, page 24). Tie off the loose threads in the inside of the nearest signature (see Tying Off the Binding, page 27) and trim the tails to ¼ inch (6 mm).

17. You will now glue the first page onto the cover. Open the front cover. Place a sheet of wax paper between the first and second pages. Using your glue brush, apply a thin layer of glue to the front of page 1.

18. Carefully remove the sheet of wax paper to avoid smearing glue onto the pages. Close the cover evenly onto page 1 to center the page as much as possible.

19. Open the cover and use a bone folder to gently smooth the page to the board **(D)**.

20. Turn the book over and attach the last page to the back cover in the same way.

21. Press the closed book beneath a heavy object (such as a large book) or in a book press for one to two hours while the glue dries.

JOURNALING INSPIRATION

Use this journal as a foundation to create a daily ritual of tea drinking and for sketching your ideas for your craft or work projects. I begin most of my days with a few moments of stillness. I've found that my best ideas arrive when I allow my mind the opportunity to rest in a quiet room with a cup of tea in my hands. I might put on soothing meditation or instrumental music and light a candle to focus my attention—but whatever you do, keep your journal and a writing utensil nearby so you can jot down inspiration when it arrives!

WEAVER OF DREAMS

WHETHER YOUR DREAMS VISIT YOU AT NIGHT OR IN THE LIGHT OF DAY,
USE THIS JOURNAL TO WEAVE THEM INTO YOUR WAKING LIFE.

Finished Dimensions

6 × 6¼ × 1½ inches (15.2 × 15.9 × 3.8 cm)

Binding Technique

Long-stitch variation (page 19)

What You Need

Basic Bookbinding Toolkit (page 11)

Bookbinding threads: two 10-inch (25.4 cm)
lengths, one 100-inch (2.5 m) length, and two
36-inch (91.4 cm) lengths

2- to 4-ounce (0.8 mm to 1.6 mm thick) leather:
17½ × 6¼ inches (44.5 × 15.9 cm) for cover and
1½ × 1½ inches (3.8 × 3.8 cm) for button

70 sheets of text-weight paper,
11½ × 6 inches (29.2 × 15.2 cm)

2 sheets of handmade paper for end sheets,
6¼ × 6 inches (15.9 × 15.2 cm)

Cardstock for templates

Lightweight wool darning thread or embroidery
thread in a variety of colors and lengths
(optional)

MAKE THE TEXT BLOCK

1. Divide the text-weight papers into groups of ten
sheets each.

2. Using a bone folder, fold the groups into signatures
measuring 5¾ × 6 inches (13.3 × 15.2 cm). You will
have a total of seven signatures. Stack them into a text
block.

3. Align the fore edge of an end sheet with the fore edge of the first signature of the text block. Wrap the sheet of handmade paper around the spine of the signature, and crease it flat with a bone folder. The overlap should be sandwiched between the first and second signatures. Repeat for the last signature.

PUNCH HOLES IN THE SIGNATURES

4. Use the cardstock to make a punch guide from Template 1. Nest the guide into the center of each signature and use an awl to punch the holes. Make sure to punch through the end sheets for the first and last signatures.

Template 1: Signature Punch Guide, 3 × 6 inches (7.6 × 15.2 cm). Enlarge template 125%.

MAKE THE COVER AND BUTTON

5. Use the cardstock to make a punch guide for the button from Template 2.

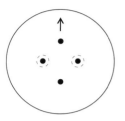

Template 2: Button Punch Guide, 1⅛ × 1⅛ inches (2.9 × 2.9 cm). Shown at full size.

6. Center Template 2 on top of the small piece of leather. With an awl, trace the outline of the template onto the leather. Using the template as a guide, mark four holes into the leather.

7. With scissors, cut out the circular piece of leather. With a ¹⁄₁₆-inch (1.6 mm) leather punch, punch the four holes. This leather circle will serve as the button for the book closure.

8. Place the piece of leather for the cover with the long edge facing you and the back side facing up. With a ruler, measure 5½ inches (14 cm) from the left edge of the cover. Use a pencil to mark this distance on the top and bottom edges (long sides).

9. Use the cardstock to make a cover punch guide from Template 3. Align the short edge of the guide to the top of the leather cover and the long edge along the pencil marks. With an awl or a pencil, mark all the holes on the template, including the ones inside the dotted circles.

Template 3: Cover Punch Guide, 6¼ × 1½ inches (15.9 × 15.9 cm). Shown at full size.

10. With a ³⁄₁₆-inch (5 mm) punch, punch the marked holes into the leather. If you're using a rotary punch, you may need to roll the edge of the leather inward to access the inner-most holes.

ATTACH THE BUTTON

11. Turn the leather cover over so that the front side of the leather is facing up. Align the two holes inside the dotted holes on the button with the two holes inside the dotted circles (on the leather Templates 2 and 3).

12. Thread a needle with one 10-inch (25.4 cm) length of binder's thread.

13. Enter the needle into one of the dotted circle holes from the inside of the cover. Draw the thread to the front of the leather and into the back side of the button. Leave a 2-inch (5.1 cm) tail of thread on the back side of the cover.

14. Draw the needle into the button hole across from the one you just exited. Pull the thread through the opposite button hole with the dotted circle and out the back side of the cover.

15. Enter into the first hole again and pull the thread to the front of the cover. Pull the thread taut. Draw the needle into the button hole across from the one you just exited to form a double stitch on the button.

16. Pull the thread to the inside of the leather cover and tie it off to the thread tail using a square knot. Trim ends to ⅛ inch (3 mm).

ASSEMBLE THE BOOK

17. Orient the cover with the back side facing up and the fore edge of the top cover facing you. Place the text block nearby with the spines facing you. Pull the bottom signature from the text block and align the sewing stations on the spine with the stations in row 1 on the cover.

18. To start sewing signature 1, thread a needle with 100 inches (2.5 m) of binder's thread. Lift the front edge of the cover and enter the needle into station 1 on the first row. Draw it through the cover and into the interior of the signature. Leave a 12-inch (30.5 cm) tail on the outside of the cover.

19. Insert the needle into station 2 and pull the thread to the outside of the cover. Then draw the needle through station 3 to the inside of the signature **(A)**.

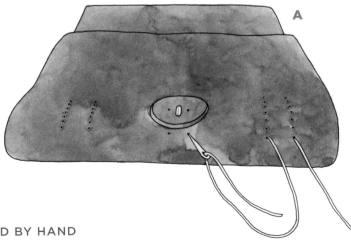

20. Draw the needle back through station 2 and pull it to the outside of the cover. Continue sewing into station 3. There will be two stitches between stations 2 and 3. Continue sewing to create two stitches between stations 4 and 5. Draw the needle through station 6 to the outside of the cover.

21. Pull the next signature from the text block and draw your needle into the nearest sewing station in the next row. Pull the thread taut through the cover and the signature. This will be a direct link—there is no need for kettle stitches. Continue sewing the remaining signatures with this long-stitch pattern variation, making two stitches between stations 2 and 3 and stations 4 and 5.

22. After you have finished attaching the last signature, place the book in an upright position. Weave the threaded needle in and out of the top stations of the cover near the head of the spine to fill in the gaps between the stations **(B)**. Tie off the end using a square knot and the trim the thread to ¼ inch (6 mm).

B

23. Thread the tail at station 1, row 1, onto the needle and repeat the method described in step 22 at the other end of the spine.

24. Thread a needle with 10 inches (25.4 cm) of binder's thread. Enter the needle into station 3 of the fourth signature from the inside of the signature. Pull it through the front of the cover and the button. Leave a 2-inch (5.1 cm) tail inside the signature.

25. Draw the needle between the two previously sewn stitches. Enter the needle into station 4 and back inside the signature **(C)**. Continue sewing to create a total of two stitches between the buttonholes at stations 3 and 4. Tie off the tail using a square knot (page 28). Trim ends to ¼ inch (6 mm).

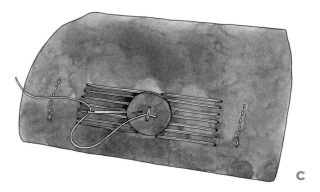

C

ATTACH THE CLOSURE

26. Wrap the cover flap around the front cover. With an awl, mark a hole onto the cover flap ¼ inch (6 mm) from the edge of the cover flap; the hole should be aligned with sewing station 4 on the spine **(D)**. Punch the hole with the leather punch.

D

27. Thread two 36-inch (91.4 cm) lengths of threads through the hole. Fold the threads over until the top and bottom ends of each thread meet.

28. Divide the threads into groups of two and simultaneously begin to twist the individual groups of thread clockwise. As the threads become twisted, begin wrapping them around each other in a counterclockwise direction. You will begin to see a twining pattern that binds the threads together into a cord **(E)**. Continue twining the threads until you have a cord that is approximately 7 inches (17.8 cm). The cord should wrap twice around the button on the spine when the book is closed and extend another 1½ inches (3.8 cm) beyond the button.

E

29. Tie off all four ends with an overhand knot (page 28). Trim the ends to ½ inch (1.3 cm).

30. Fasten the journal by closing the flap and wrapping the twined cord twice around the button.

EMBELLISH THE BINDING (OPTIONAL)

31. Thread a binder's needle with the thread of your choice. The length of your thread should be at least 10 inches (25.4 cm).

32. Place the book in an upright position. Starting near the button on the spine, weave your thread over and under each set of double stitches at one side of the spine. Leave a 1-inch (2.5 cm) tail.

33. When you're about to run out of your thread, remove the needle and leave at least 1 inch (2.5 cm) of thread hanging from the edge of your weaving.

34. Thread your needle with a second color of thread. Continue weaving from where you left off. Leave a tail of thread hanging off the edge at the end and beginning of the second weave. Continue adding threads in this way. You can experiment with weaving patterns by moving your needle over and under two sets of double stitches at a time instead.

35. Secure the loose ends by pairing them up and tying them together with a simple square knot (page 28). Don't cinch the knot too tight, or otherwise it will pull on the weaving.

36. Trim the ends to ¼ inch (6 mm). With your bone folder, push them beneath your woven thread to hide them from sight.

37. Repeat steps 31–36 to add weaving to the other side of the spine, if desired.

JOURNALING INSPIRATION

Keep a pen and book beside your bed and record your dreams immediately upon waking while the impressions are still vivid. What did your dream feel like? Did you experience a particular emotion or challenge? Do you notice your dreams are easier to remember with practice? Alternatively, you can use this book to write down your daydreams or any illuminating ideas that visit in the daytime.

LIGHT AND SHADOW

IT IS EASY TO ACCEPT THE BRIGHTNESS AND GOODNESS OF LIFE, BUT HOW ABOUT OUR CHALLENGES AND MORE SHADOWY NATURES? USE THIS JOURNAL TO HOUSE THE DUALITY OF YOUR LIFE EXPERIENCES.

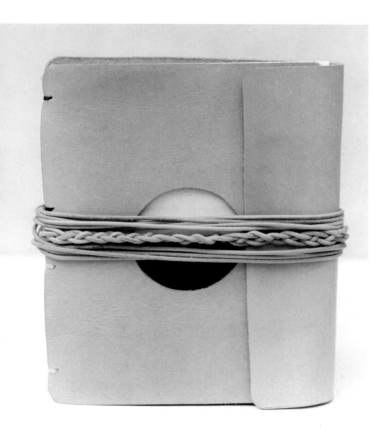

What You Need

Basic Bookbinding Toolkit (page 11)

Black bookbinding thread, 45 inches (114 cm)

White bookbinding thread, 45 inches (114 cm)

70 sheets of black text-weight paper, 10 × 3 inches (25.4 × 7.6 cm)

70 sheets of white text-weight paper, 10 × 3 inches (25.4 × 7.6 cm)

1 strip of black text-weight paper, 10 × ½ inches (25.4 × 7.6 cm)

1 strip of white text-weight paper, 10 × ½ inches (25.4 × 7.6 cm)

Cardstock for templates

2- to 4-ounce (0.8 to 1.6 mm thick) leather: 5 × 6¼ inches (12.7 × 15.9 cm) for front cover, and 7½ × 6¼ inches (19 × 15.9 cm) for back cover

Four ⅛-inch (3 mm) thick leather cords, 40 inches long (102 cm) each

Finished Dimensions

5 ½ × 6¼ × 1 inches (14 × 15.9 × 2.5 cm)

Binding Techniques

Running stitch (page 18)

True kettle stitch (page 23)

ASSEMBLE THE TEXT BLOCKS

1. Divide the sheets of white text-weight paper into groups of 10 sheets each. Use a bone folder to fold each group into a signature measuring 5 × 3 inches (12.7 × 7.6 cm). You will have a total of 7 signatures. Repeat for the black papers.

2. Stack the signatures into two text blocks by color.

3. Make a punch guide from Template 1 on the cardstock. Nest the guide into the center of each signature. With the awl, punch all four holes in each signature. Stack the signatures into text blocks, one white and one black, with the spines facing you **(A)**.

A

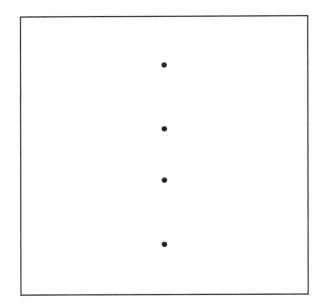

Template 1: Signature Punch Guide, 3 × 3 inches (7.6 × 7.6 cm). Shown at full size.

4. Position the white paper strip horizontally on your work surface. Fold the strip in half to create a narrower strip of paper measuring 10 × ¼ inches (25.4 × 0.6 cm). Repeat for the black paper strip.

5. Wrap the folded white strip around the spine edge of the white text block and the black strip around the spine of the black text block **(B)**. The width of the strips should fit between the two center sewing stations of the text blocks. There should be an equal length of paper folded on the front and back of each text block.

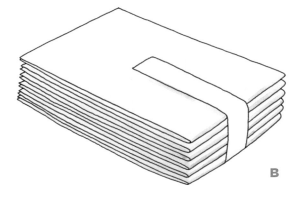

B

MAKE THE COVERS

6. Create a punch guide from Template 2 using the cardstock. With a ¼-inch (6 mm) hole punch, punch out the center hole in the circle.

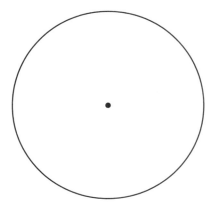

Template 2: Cover Circle Punch Guide, 2 × 2 inches (5.1 × 5.1 cm). Shown at full size.

7. Place the piece of leather for the front cover on your work surface, with the outside facing up. Locate the center of the leather with a ruler and mark the center with an awl.

8. Align Template 2 over the front cover leather so the mark is beneath the center hole in the template. With an awl, trace the outer edge of the circle onto the front cover. Fold the leather cover in half. With scissors, make a 1-inch (2.5 cm) cut inside the circle **(C)**. This will allow you to carefully cut along the circle outline to make a window into the front cover **(D)**.

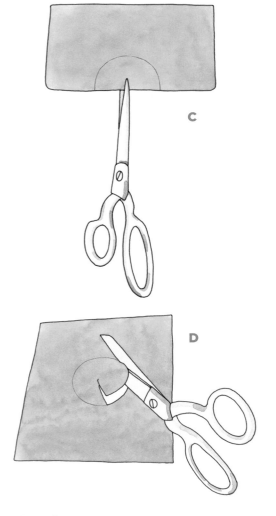

Optional: Round all four corners of each cover with a corner round or by hand with scissors.

ASSEMBLE THE BOOK

9. Position the black text block with the punched spine facing in your direction.

10. Thread a needle with white thread. Pull a signature from the top of the stack.

11. Enter the needle into the sewing station farthest to your right (station 1). Draw the thread to the inside of the signature, leaving a 12-inch (30.5 cm) tail on the outside of the cover. Enter the needle into the next sewing station (station 2) and pull the thread to outside the cover.

12. Enter the needle into the third sewing station. Pull the thread to the inside of the signature, leaving a small loop of thread between the two center stations.

13. Place the black paper strip through the loop. Tighten the thread so the strip rests flat against the signature. Continue sewing the rest of the signature using the running stitch.

14. Pull the next signature from the text block and directly link it to the previous one by entering the needle into the far left sewing station of the new signature. Continue sewing the signature the same way as with signature 1, making a running stitch over the paper strip. Link the thread to the loose tail at the sewing station farthest to the right on signature 1 with a square knot.

15. Continue sewing the rest of the text block using the running stitch, adding the signatures and sewing over the paper strip in the center as before. Link the top stations of the signatures together using a true kettle stitch (page 23) between each pair as you work. Link the bottom stations of the signatures together in the same way. The stitches between the center sewing stations should sit over the strip of paper (see page 18 for more information about sewing over tapes).

Tip: Once you have sewn a new signature in place (but before you link it with a true kettle stitch), press the signature down near the center strip. This will decrease the space between the signatures and help create a tight, firm binding.

16. Once you make the final true kettle stitch on the seventh signature, leave the needle on the thread and set the text block to the side.

17. Thread a new needle with black thread. Repeat steps 11–15 to sew the white text block together. When you are finished, leave the needle on the thread **(E)**.

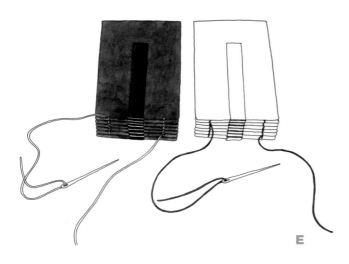

E

PUNCH HOLES IN THE COVERS

18. Place the white text block in front of you with the spine facing in your direction. Set the black text block to the right of the white one; the edges of the text blocks should touch. Place the front cover (with the circle window) on top of the text blocks, aligning all the edges. Slide the 7½ × 6¼–inch (19 × 15.9 cm) piece of leather beneath the text blocks so any excess width extends beyond the fore edges of the front cover and text blocks. Check that the spine edges are even with one another.

19. With an awl, mark four sewing stations into the top cover, ¼ inch (6 mm) in from the spine edge. The cover holes should align with the first and last sewing stations of each text block **(F)**. Punch the holes with a ¹⁄₁₆ inch (1.6 mm) leather hole punch.

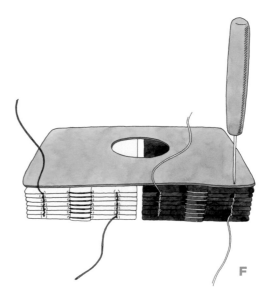

F

20. Place the back cover on your worktable with the back side facing up. Using the punched holes in the front cover as a guide, mark the holes from the front cover onto the back cover with an awl.

21. Punch the holes in the back cover with a leather hole punch.

ATTACH THE COVERS

22. Return both covers to the text block. Align the text block so the spine faces you. Remove the black text block and set it to the side. Attach the top cover to the top left sewing station of the white text block using the needle threaded with black thread (page 24).

23. Once you have linked the top cover to the white text block at the hole on your left, hike your thread (page 24) down the stitches on the far left stations of the text block. When you reach the bottom signature, attach the bottom cover also. Then enter the needle into the nearest sewing station of the bottom signature of the white text block and tie off the loose threads on the inside of the signature with a square knot (page 28). Trim the thread ends to ¼ inch (6 mm).

24. Turn the book over and thread a needle to the tail of thread on the other end of the white signature. Attach the front and back covers to the white text block by repeating steps 22 and 23.

Tip: Try not to attach the covers too tightly, or they will pull too far down the spine. Leave a little slack in the thread and make sure the cover opens and closes easily.

25. Place the black text block next to the white text block inside the covers. Attach the black text block to the cover in the same way you attached the white text block.

ATTACH THE TIE

26. Tuck all edges of the pages neatly into the cover. Push the text blocks together—the edges of the white and black text blocks should be flush against each other in the circle window.

27. Make a punch guide from Template 3 on cardstock.

28. Center the punch guide (Template 3) on the back cover, positioning the SPINE label closest to the spine.

29. With an awl, mark the holes onto the back cover. Punch the holes into the cover with a ⅛-inch (3 mm) leather punch. You will be attaching four cords to the back cover in these punched holes.

Tip: To punch holes in the cover with a rotary punch, you may need to roll the wraparound edge to gain access to the place for the holes.

30. Tie an overhand knot (page 28) ½ inch (1.3 cm) from one end of each leather cord.

31. Starting from the outside of the cover, insert the loose end of one cord into one of the four holes nearest the cover spine. Pull the cord to the inside of the cover until the knot rests firmly against the leather.

32. From the inside of the cover, thread the cord into the closest hole on the next row of 4 holes, and pull the cord to the outside of the cover.

33. Continue threading the remaining three leather cords onto the back cover in this way. The loose ends of the cord should all be running away from the spine of the cover **(G)**. With scissors, trim the tail ends of the leather cords with knots to ⅛ inch (3 mm).

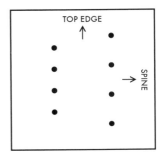

Template 3: Tie Attachment Punch Guide, 1½ × 1½ inches (3.8 × 3.8 cm). Shown at full size.

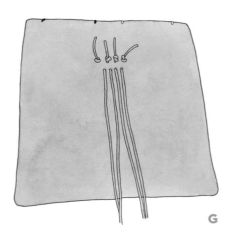

G

Optional: Use the cords to make a four-stranded braid (page 47). Secure the finished braid by wrapping binding thread around the ends of the four cords, using the same technique featured in step 19 of The Herbalist (page 69).

34. To close the journal, wrap the flap of the back cover around the front cover, align all paper edges, and wrap the cords around the book several times. Secure the cords by tucking the ends beneath previously wrapped rounds of cord. You can choose to trim the cords shorter so that you do not have to wrap your journal as many times—it's up to you!

JOURNALING INSPIRATION

Fill one side of the journal with thoughts of positivity and lightness and the other side with thoughts that feel heavy and shadowy. How do you honor the lightness of your being? How do you honor your shadows and darkness? How do you integrate these dualities to honor your whole experience? Illuminate your insights by writing with a metallic paint pen. Write titles for the two sections onto the paper strips in the front of the book, such as "Book of Shadow" and "Book of Light" or "I Am Made of Shadow" and "I Am Made of Light."

FOUR-STRAND BRAIDING

Making a four-strand braid isn't much more difficult than braiding with three strands. The extra strand just takes a little getting used to! Use this braid to make a unique and textured wraparound tie for your journal.

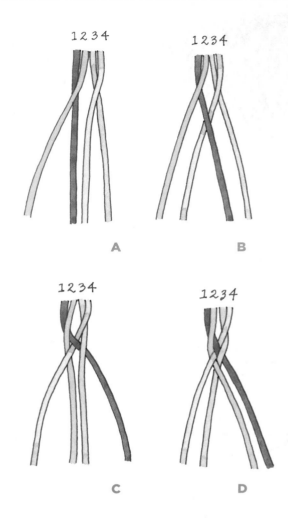

WHAT YOU NEED

4 cords or threads of equal length

1. Secure the end of each strand using the method suggested in your project.

2. Cross the cord in position 2 over the cord in position 1 and the cord in position 4 over the cord in position 3 **(A)**.

3. Cross the cord in position 2 over the cord in position 3 **(B)**.

4. Repeat steps 2 and 3 until the braid reaches the desired length **(C and D)**.

5. Bind the cord ends together by making a loop knot (page 28) or by wrapping binding thread around them and tying it off.

THE ART OF REPETITION

THROUGH RHYTHM AND REPETITION, WE CAN LEARN TO STILL OUR MINDS AND ACCESS THE PRESENT MOMENT. PRACTICE BECOMING AWARE OF YOUR BREATH WHILE STITCHING THIS SIMPLE BOOKLET.

Finished Dimensions

4 × 5 × ¾ inches (10.2 × 12.7 × 1.9 cm)

Binding Techniques

Running-stitch variation
(page 18)

What You Need

Basic Bookmaking Toolkit (page 11)

Bookbinding thread, 18 inches (45.7 cm)

1 piece of denim from a recycled pair of jeans, 8 × 5 inches (20.3 × 12.7 cm)

3 pieces of boiled wool or cotton flannel: 7½ × 4½ inches (19.1 × 11.4 cm), 7 × 4 inches (17.8 × 10.2 cm), and 6½ × 3½ inches (16.5 × 8.9 cm)

4 dressmaker's pins

Masking tape

MAKE THE SIGNATURES

1. In this project, fabric takes the place of paper and board. Stack all four pieces of fabric according to size, from largest to smallest. The large denim piece will form the cover of the book and should be on the bottom, with the inside of the fabric facing up. The smallest piece of wool or flannel will become the center of the signature and should be on the top of the stack.

2. Using the dressmaker's pins, pin the stack together near its horizontal edges. Use a ruler to find the fold line and mark it by sticking a piece of masking tape to the left edge of the line. This is where the spine of the book will be located.

ASSEMBLE THE BOOK

3. Thread a needle with bookbinding thread and enter the needle from the inside of the signature into the center point of the fold line, next to the right edge of the tape. Pull the needle through each layer of fabric, leaving a tail of 3 inches (7.6 cm) of thread on the inside of the signature.

4. Move the needle down ¼ inch (6 mm) and enter the needle into the cover at this point. Pull the thread to the inside of the signature. Continue sewing in running stitch, spacing the stitches approximately ¼ inch (6 mm) apart, until you reach the bottom edge of the second-largest piece of fabric. From there, begin guiding the needle and thread upwards in running stitch to fill in the gaps between the previous stitches.

Tip: Each time the tip of your needle touches the fabric, pause and take a breath. Once your lungs feel naturally full, draw the thread to the other side of the fabric and release your breath as you pull the thread to its length. Repeat for 10 stitches. Let this mindfulness practice seep into your other projects—if you notice your body becoming tense or find yourself holding your breath, remember to pause and breathe.

5. Once you return to the center point of the signature, continue sewing upwards until you reach the top edge of the second largest layer **(A)**. From there, return to the center point using running stitch, filling in the gaps between the stitches you have just sewn.

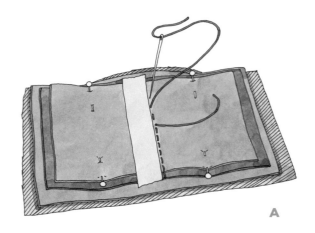

A

6. When you arrive at the center point again, tie off the loose threads (page 27) in the inside of the signature and trim the thread tails to ½ inch (1.3 cm). Remove the tape and pins.

JOURNALING INSPIRATION

Fill the pages with embroidery motifs or stitches using leftover thread from sewing projects. You can make up your own designs and stitches or find inspiration with the ones featured on pages 50–51.

ORNAMENTAL STITCHES

Add texture to the covers or cloth pages of your book with these ornamental stitches. The weaving stitch is commonly used for darning holes. The running stitch is a commonly used embroidery stitch called by many names (e.g., straight stitch, basic weave, sashiko, kantha), depending on where you live in the world and what type of craft you are applying it to.

WHAT YOU NEED

Embroidery thread

Embroidery needle

Scissors

Fabric cover or 1- to 2-ounce (0.4 mm to 0.8 mm thick) leather

WEAVING STITCH

1. Thread your needle with a 12-inch (30.5 cm) piece of thread and allow for a 2-inch (5 cm) tail.

2. Tie a square knot (page 28) onto the long end of your thread.

3. Enter your needle into the back side of the fabric cover and pull the full length of the thread to the front until the square knot is resting against the wrong side of the fabric.

4. Make a vertical stitch on the front of the fabric by inserting the needle 1 inch (2.5 cm) from the entry point and drawing the thread to the back side.

5. To make a second vertical stitch on the front of your fabric, insert the needle ⅛ inch (3 mm) to the left of the first stitch on the back of the fabric and draw the thread to the front of the fabric. Bring the needle down 1 inch (2.5 cm) and draw the needle to the back of the fabric at this point **(A)**.

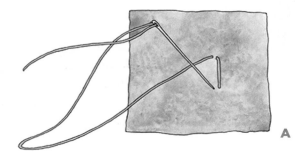

A

6. Continue making vertical stitches in this pattern until you have a total of six stitches on the front of the fabric.

7. On the back side of the fabric, tie off the thread with a square knot. To form the square knot, slip your needle underneath the nearest stitch to form a loop and insert your needle through the loop then tighten. Repeat once to secure knot. Trim the tails to ⅛ inch (3 mm).

8. Thread your needle with another 12-inch (30.5 cm) thread in the same or complementary color. Tie a square knot on the long end.

9. Enter the needle into the back side of the fabric ⅛ inch (3 mm) to the right of the vertical thread. Pull the thread through to the front of the fabric until the square knot is pressed against the back side of the fabric.

10. Weave your needle over and under all six vertical stitches and pull the thread through. Enter into the fabric ⅛ inch (3 mm) to the left of the last vertical thread and pull through to the back side of the fabric.

11. Draw the needle up ⅛ inch (3 mm) and enter into the fabric from the back. Pull the thread through to the front. This time, weave in the opposite manner and direction to the first time—go over the sixth thread, under the fifth, over the fourth, etc.—and pull the thread through **(B)**.

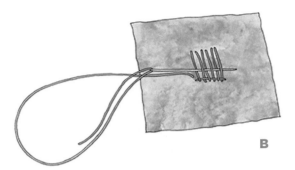

B

12. Enter the fabric and draw the needle to the back side of the fabric.

13. Continue stitching and weaving the thread in this way until you reach the top of the vertical stitches.

14. Draw the thread to the back. Tie off the loose thread with a square knot (page 28) Trim the tails to ⅛ inch (3 mm).

RUNNING STITCH

1. Thread your needle with a 20-inch (50.8 cm) piece of thread.

2. Tie a square knot onto the long end of your thread, leaving a short tail of thread.

3. Enter into the back side of the fabric and pull the full length of thread to the front until the square knot is resting against the back of the fabric.

4. Insert the needle ⅛ inch (3 mm) from the entry point and weave the needle through the fabric in ⅛-inch (3 mm) increments, continuing in the same direction **(C)**. Pull the thread through the new stitches until it is taut.

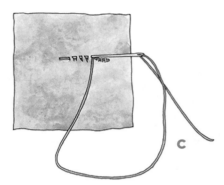

C

5. Continue weaving your needle along your stitching path until you reach the end of your first row of running stitches.

6. When you are ready to start the next row of stitching, draw the needle to the back side and pull the thread taut. Insert the needle ⅛ inch (3 mm) above your last stitch and pull it to the front.

7. Continue weaving your needle parallel to the first row to make a new row of stitches, using the running stitch.

8. When your pattern is complete, draw thread to the back side of the fabric. Insert your needle under the nearest stitch without pushing your needle to the front side and tie off the loose thread with a square knot. Trim the tails to ⅛ inch (3 mm).

GARLAND OF GRATITUDE

WHAT ARE YOU THANKFUL FOR TODAY? MAKE TIME EACH DAY TO
SEW SIGNATURES TO YOUR JOURNAL AND RECORD YOUR GRATITUDE.
BY THE YEAR'S END, YOU'LL HAVE A GARLAND'S WORTH OF THINGS
TO BE GRATEFUL FOR.

Finished Dimensions

3 × 3 × 60 inches (7.6 × 7.6 × 152.4 cm)

Binding Techniques

Double French stitch (page 23)

What You Need

Basic Bookbinding Toolkit (page 11)

Bookbinding thread, 54 inches (137.2 cm) to start

¾-inch (1.9 cm) wide ribbon or bias tape,
60 inches (152.4 cm)

730 sheets of text-weight paper in a variety of
colors, 3 × 6 inches (7.6 × 15.2 cm)

Cardstock for template

1 container or shoe box for storage

MAKE THE TEXT BLOCK

1. Divide the text-weight paper into multiple piles. Organize the piles with a mix of colors that appeal to you; it doesn't matter how many sheets are in each one. Pull two sheets from each stack and pair them together. Using your bone folder, fold the two sheets into a single signature that measures 3 × 3 inches (7.6 × 7.6 cm). Repeat until you have 365 signatures, or one for each day you intend to record what you're thankful for.

2. Place 14 signatures onto your work surface. Place the remaining signatures in a shoe box or storage container to attach later.

PUNCH HOLES IN THE SIGNATURES

3. Create a punch guide from cardstock using Template 1.

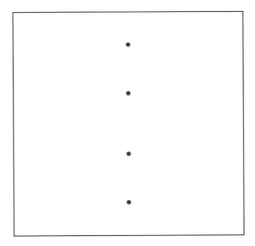

Template 1: Signature Punch Guide, 3 × 3 inches (7.6 × 7.6 cm). Enlarge template 125%.

4. Nest the punch guide into the center of one of the signatures. Using an awl, punch the sewing stations into the signature. Repeat for all 13 of the remaining signatures on your table. Store the punch guide in the box along with the remaining signatures for later use.

ASSEMBLE THE BOOK

5. To prepare the text block for binding, make certain all the pages of the 14 signatures are in order with signature 1 (the first pages of your book) on top. The spines of the signatures should be facing you. Now turn the stack over so the first signature is on the bottom of the stack.

6. Pull signature 1 from the bottom of the stack. Thread the needle with bookbinding thread. Begin binding signature 1 from the outside. Insert the needle and bookbinding thread into sewing station 1 (the rightmost station) and draw it out through sewing station 2, leaving a tail of 4 inches (10.2 cm) of loose thread hanging from the first station. Next, insert the needle and thread into sewing station 3 and draw it out again through station 4.

7. Set the needle down and pull the ribbon underneath the stitch between stations 2 and 3. Leave approximately 20 inches (50.8 cm) of ribbon to hang off the front of signature 1. Pull the thread taut between all the stations.

8. Pull signature 2 from the bottom of the stack and place it on top of signature 1. Insert the thread directly into station 4 from the outside and draw it out through sewing station 3 of signature 2. Link the center stitches of signatures 1 and 2 together with a double French stitch (page 23) by wrapping the working thread twice around the center stitch of the previous signature. Using the "sewing over tapes" method (page 18), sew over the ribbon and into station 2 of signature 2, then out of station 1. Link station 1 of signatures 1 and 2 together with a square knot.

9. Continue sewing the text block together, one signature at a time, in the same way, using the sewing-over-tapes method, with double French stitches (page 23) between stations 2 and 3. Link the signatures together at stations 1 and 4 with true kettle stitches **(A)**.

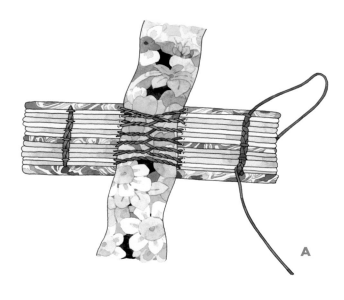

10. Once you have 6 inches (15.2 cm) remaining on your thread, allow it to dangle from the binding from the most recently completed true kettle stitch for an organic, playful look, or tie it off on the inside with a square knot (page 28) and trim.

ADDING NEW SIGNATURES

11. When you're ready to add new signatures, anchor a new 54-inch (137 cm) length of thread (page 29) and continue adding signatures. You can change thread colors to provide more visual interest when adding a new group of signatures. Stitch as many signatures as you want when you have to refill pages. Each 54-inch (137 cm) length of thread will stitch about 14 signatures, but feel free to experiment with the length of thread to change the thread color more often. Once you have completed the garland, simply allow your thread to dangle at the final kettle stitch or tie off on the inside of the last signature and trim.

A

JOURNALING INSPIRATION

Reflect on your life. Can you find things to be thankful for even when you're facing challenges? Can you see the light in the darkness? How do you make lemonade from the sour or bitter experiences that show up in your life? Each day, record your gratitude in a new signature and then sew it to the text block. Decorate your pages by adding newspaper clippings, receipts, artwork, drawings, and lightly applied watercolor to the signatures. Make it a collaborative project by inviting your friends or family to join in! When it's complete, hang the book on a wall in your home for a continual reminder of everything you have to be grateful for.

FOLLOW YOUR TRUTH

THERE ARE MANY TRUTHS TO GUIDE YOU THROUGH LIFE. REMEMBER YOURS BY USING THIS JOURNAL TO MAKE A COLLECTION OF CONCEPTS, IDEAS, AND QUOTES THAT RING TRUE TO YOU.

Finished Dimensions

8 × 2 × 1¾ inches (20.3 × 5.1 × 4.4 cm)

Binding Technique

Post bound (page 7)

What You Need

Basic Bookbinding Toolkit (page 11)

120 sheets scrapbook weight paper, 8 × 2 inches (20.3 × 5.1 cm)

2 sheets of decorative handmade paper, 8 × 2 inches (20.3 × 5.1 cm)

Cardstock for template

2- to 4-ounce (0.8 to 1.6 mm thick) leather: 8 × 2 inches (20.3 × 5.1 cm) for front cover, and 13½ × 2 inches (34.3 × 5.1 cm) for back cover

⅛-inch (3 mm) thick leather cord, 45 inches (114.3 cm) long for tie

Binding post, 3⁄16 × 1½ inches (5 mm × 3.8 cm)

MAKE THE TEXT BLOCK

1. Stack all sheets into one text block, placing the decorative end pages on the top and bottom.

2. Create a punch guide from Template 1 on cardstock and punch the hole.

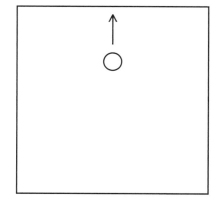

Template 1: Signature Punch Guide, 2 × 2 inches (5.1 × 5.1 cm). Shown at full size.

3. Position the template on the short end of the top page of the text block. Align the edge of the template with the top edge of the page, with the template's arrow pointing up. Using a pen, mark the hole onto the top page and then punch the hole through one page. Continue using the top page as a guide to punch the remaining papers, five to ten pages at a time.

MAKE THE COVER

4. You will use the original top page you used to punch the paper to punch the cover so all the punched holes will align. Line up the punched edge of the paper with a short edge of the 8 × 2–inch (20.3 × 5.1 cm) piece of leather. This will be the front cover. Mark the hole on the leather with an awl and punch a hole into the leather with the leather punch. Repeat this step to punch a hole in one short end of the 13½ × 2–inch (34.3 × 5.1 cm) piece of leather, which will form the back cover. The unpunched end of the back cover will wrap around the end of the text block and up to the front.

Optional: Ink the edges of your text block (page 57).

ASSEMBLE THE BOOK

5. Unscrew the binding post. Set the bolt of the post in front of you with the post pointing upwards.

6. Push the hole on the front cover onto the post, with the cover's front side facing down. Then push five to ten sheets of the text block on top of the post. Continue gradually placing the remaining pages and then the back cover onto the post. The back cover should face up **(A)**. Once the entire text block is fastened to the post, screw the head of the binding the post back onto the bolt.

ATTACH THE TIE

7. Turn the book over. Align it vertically on your worktable with the binding post at the top. Wrap the end of the back cover around the end of the text block and rest it on top of the front cover.

8. With an awl, mark a hole onto the wraparound flap ½ inch (1.2 cm) from the corner edge of the wraparound flap **(B)**. Punch a hole at the mark, using the leather punch.

B

9. Make an overhand knot on one end of the leather cord (page 28). Starting from the outside of the cover, thread the loose end of the cord through the hole in the cover until the knot catches on the outside of the cover. To hold the journal closed, wrap the cord several times around the journal and secure the end by tucking it beneath the wrapped section of cord.

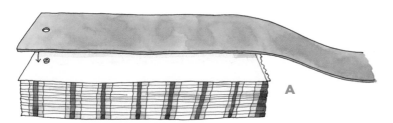

A

INKED EDGES

WHAT YOU NEED

Unbound text block with smooth edges

Thick, wide rubber band

Sandpaper, medium or fine grit

India ink

Gold paint pen

Paintbrush

Wax paper

1. Place the wax paper on your work surface to protect it from ink.

2. Secure your text block with a thick rubber band. Make sure all the edges of the paper are even. If your pages are hand cut, it's okay if some of the edges stick out a little.

3. With the sandpaper, smooth all four edges of the text block. Shake or blow the paper dust off in a well-ventilated area.

4. Hold the text block securely in one hand, pressing the pages together tightly. With your other hand, dip the paintbrush into the India ink and apply a pattern of vertical and horizontal brushstrokes to the edges of the text block. You're painting freehand, so don't worry if they are uneven. Then outline the brushstrokes with a gold paint pen. You may need to shift the placement of the rubber band to ink the areas underneath it.

5. Set the text block down and allow it dry for 10 to 15 minutes. Once dry to the touch, remove the rubber band. You can create a static pattern by rearranging groups of 10 to 15 pages. Once you're satisfied with the design, return the text block between the covers for binding.

JOURNALING INSPIRATION

Sit for a few minutes in a quiet room. Ask yourself, "What do I believe in? What is true to me?" Begin a list of ideas that come to you. Consider whether they are true by the way your body or heart feels when you repeat them to yourself. Look for a subtle opening or expansive sensation if the idea resonates, or an indifferent or contracting sensation if it does not. Alternatively, carry this book with you to record quotes and ideas that resonate with you through the day. Then, find a quiet space to sit with the ideas and reflect on them through journaling.

JOURNALS for EVERYDAY LIVING

THE MAKER

BUILDERS AND DIYers OF THE WORLD—USE THIS BOOK, WITH ITS BUILT-IN PENCIL HOLDER, FOR JOTTING DOWN NOTES AND MEASUREMENTS OR FOR CAPTURING YOUR IDEAS WHILE YOU'RE ON THE GO.

Finished Dimensions

3½ × 6 × ¾ inches (8.9 × 15.2 × 2 cm)

Binding Technique

Pamphlet stitch (page 18)

What You Need

Basic Bookmaking Toolkit (page 11)

Bookbinding thread, two 18-inch (45.7 cm)
   lengths

24 sheets of text-weight paper,
   3½ × 11 inches (8.9 × 28 cm)

Cardstock for template

2- to 3-ounce (0.8 to 1.2 mm thick) leather: 3½ ×
   12 inches (8.9 × 30.5 cm) for the cover and
   3½ × 1½ inches (8.9 × 3.8 cm) for the pencil
   holder

Writing implement for book

Thin hair elastic

MAKE THE SIGNATURES

1. Divide the text-weight paper into two stacks of
twelve sheets each. Fold each stack into a signature
that measures 3½ × 5½ inches (8.9 × 14 cm) using a
bone folder to smooth the thick folded edge.

PUNCH THE SEWING STATIONS

2. Create a signature punch guide on cardstock using
Template 1.

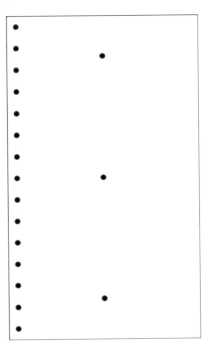

*Template 1: Signature Punch Guide, 3½ × 2 inches
(8.9 × 5.1 cm). Shown at full size.*

3. Nest the punch guide inside one of the signatures
and place the signature in the gutter of an open phone
book. Punch the three center holes with the awl **(A)**.
Repeat for the other signature.

A

4. Nest one signature inside the other. You will now have one thick signature with 96 pages.

MAKE THE COVER

5. Place the leather pieces on your work surface with the back sides facing up. The short edges of both pieces of leather for the cover should be parallel to the edge of your work table.

6. Fold the large piece of leather in half crosswise. Mark the center fold on the back side with your pencil. Align the center hole on the punch guide on the center fold on the leather. Use your awl to mark all three holes in the middle of the template onto the center fold. Set the large piece of leather aside.

7. Fold the small leather piece in half lengthwise, and mark this fold line on the back side of the piece with your pencil. Align the punch guide on the fold line you just drew and on the short edges of the leather. Use your awl to mark the three spaced holes onto the leather. This piece will become the pencil holder.

8. Punch holes at the marks on both pieces of leather with the ³⁄₃₂-inch (24 mm) leather punch. These will be the sewing stations that join pages, cover, and pencil holder together.

ASSEMBLE THE BOOK

9. Thread your needle with one 18-inch (45.7 cm) piece of thread. Place the leather cover piece on your work surface with the back side facing up. Place the folded signature along the holes in the leather so that the sewing stations on the leather and signature align. Fold the leather cover over the signature. Place the small piece of leather with its front side facing the large leather cover so its sewing stations align also.

10. Open the signature and guide the threaded needle into the center hole. Draw the needle through the signature, the leather cover, and the small leather piece

until 3 inches (7.6 cm) of loose thread remain on the inside of the signature **(B)**.

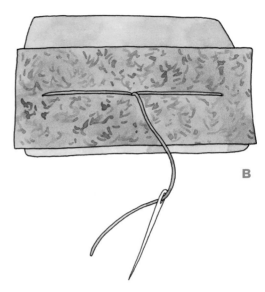

B

11. Continue sewing with the pamphlet stitch method (see page 18). Be sure to sew all three layers together at each sewing station. Tie off inside the signature near the center hole (see Tying Off the Binding, page 27). Trim the threads to ¼ inch (6 mm).

ASSEMBLE THE PENCIL HOLDER

12. Nest the writing implement inside the small piece of leather. Firmly press the edges of the leather around the width of the implement and use a pencil to mark the points where one edge of the leather meets the other. Remove the writing implement and place the book on your work surface. Align a ruler to the pencil mark on one side of the leather piece and draw an even trim line along the long edge of the small piece of leather. Repeat on the other long edge. With scissors, cut away the excess leather, using the trim lines as a guide.

13. Place the edge of the punch guide with the line of holes next to one long edge of the leather strip that will hold the writing implement. Use a pencil and the edge dots on the template to mark holes ⅛ inch (3 mm) in from the edge of the leather **(C)**. Repeat on the other long edge of the pencil holder. Use the ¹⁄₁₆-inch (1.6 mm) hole punch to punch new holes.

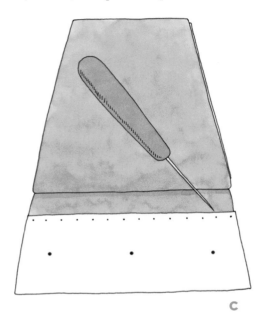

C

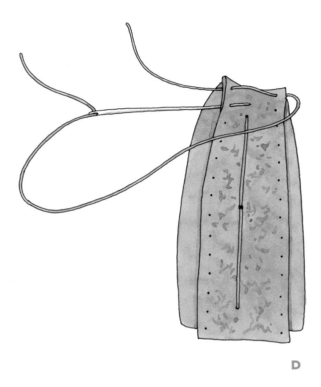

D

14. Thread the other 18-inch (45.7 cm) thread with one needle on each end. Leave a 1-inch (2.5 cm) tail on each side.

15. Place the book inside a book press or between your knees with the spine facing outward.

16. Guide one needle into the upper rightmost hole on the pencil holder and the other needle into the upper leftmost hole of the pencil holder. Pull both needles through until the thread is taut and evenly distributed on both sides.

17. Guide the needle on the right side around the outer right edge of the pencil holder and into the second hole on the front side of the left leather piece **(D)**. Pick up the other needle and guide it around the outer left edge of the leather and into the second hole on the front side of the right leather piece (like lacing a pair of boots). Evenly pull both needles until the thread is taut and both leather edges firmly meet.

18. Place your writing implement inside the newly forming holder and again pull the threads taut.

19. Continue sewing in this pattern, crisscrossing stitches by guiding the needles down to the opposite open hole on the leather and pulling the thread taut around the implement. You will notice a V-shaped stitching pattern begin to appear.

20. Once you reach the end of stitching the pencil holder, pull the threads to the underside of the leather to hide them. Tie both ends together using a square knot (page 28) **(E)**. Trim the thread ends to ¹⁄₁₆ inch (1.6 mm).

E

TRIM THE COVERS

21. Place the book on your work surface. Lift the front cover and press down evenly on the text block so it aligns with the cover edges. If there is excess leather beyond the fore edge of the signature, use a pencil to trace the edge of the signature onto the leather. With scissors, trim off the excess leather from the cover. Repeat on the other cover.

ATTACH THE CLOSURE

22. Position the closed book so the back cover is facing up. Use a ruler to mark two holes 1¼ inches (3.2 cm) from the fore edge of the cover and centered between the long cover edges. The marks should have a ¼-inch (6 mm) space between them. Punch the marks with the ⅛-inch (3 mm) leather hole punch.

23. Open the back cover of the book. Guide the hair elastic through one of the holes in the back cover so it pokes through to the outside of the cover. Repeat for the other end of the tie and the other hole. Both ends of the tie should appear on the outside of the cover, one through each hole.

24. Guide one loop of the hair elastic through the loop on the other side and pull it taut so the tie wraps around the holes on the leather cover **(F)**.

25. Securely close the journal by stretching the open loop of the hair band around the entire bottom portion of the book.

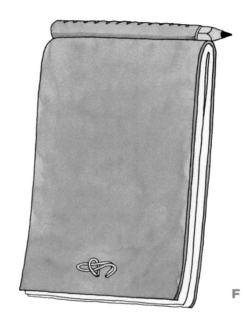

F

JOURNALING INSPIRATION

When you find yourself stuck when you're working on a project, fill a page or two with any ideas that come to mind. Let your thoughts flow as if you were speaking to a friend, no matter how nonsensical they might seem. Sometimes solutions are sparked by the most unlikely phrase or word. You can also use this book to store ideas for your up-and-coming works of art.

THE HERBALIST

FOR LOVERS OF FLORA—PROTECT YOUR FIELD OBSERVATIONS, WATERCOLORS, AND HARVESTING NOTES INSIDE THIS RUSTIC-HEWN BOOK.

Finished Dimensions

4 × 7½ × 1¾ inches (10.1 × 19 × 4.4 cm)

Binding Techniques

Running stitch (page 18)

What You Need

Basic Bookbinding Toolkit (page 11)

Bookbinding thread, 112 inches (284.5 cm)

21 sheets of 90 lb. (190 gsm) hot-pressed
watercolor paper, 7¾ × 7 inches
(19.7 × 17.8 cm)

7 sheets of deckle-edge handmade paper,
8 × 7 inches (20.3 × 17.8 cm)

Cardstock for template

2 wooden boards, 4 × 7½ × ⅜ inches
(10.1 × 19 × 1 cm)

Jute cord, ¼-inch (6 mm) thick, 60 inches
(1.5 m)

Handheld drill with a ³⁄₁₆-inch (5 mm)
wood bit

Scrap wood board

Dust mask

Note: I advise being in a well-ventilated area and
using a dust mask for at least the drilling portion
of this project in order to avoid breathing in
sawdust.

MAKE THE COVERS

1. Create a punch guide from Template 1 using
cardstock. Fold it in half vertically and sandwich it
between the cover boards. Align the punch marks
with the long edge of the board.

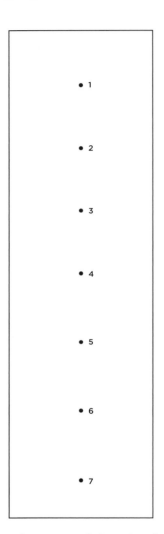

*Template 1: Signature and Cover Punch Guide, 2 × 7
inches (5 × 18 cm). Enlarge template 133%.*

2. Slide one of the cover boards ¼ inch (6 mm) away from the folded edge of the guide so that the sewing stations are visible. Make certain that the guide is vertically centered within the edges of the board.

3. With a pencil, mark the top and bottom sewing stations on the cover board **(A)**. The marks should be ¼ inch (6 mm) in from the spine edge. Flip the stack over and repeat for the bottom board. Each board will have two marks.

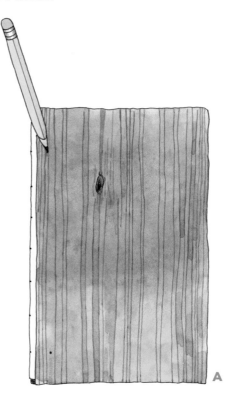

A

4. Move to a well-ventilated work area, and put on the dust mask to protect your lungs and the safety glasses to protect your eyes from the sawdust.

5. Place one of the boards on the piece of scrap wood. With a handheld drill, make holes through the two marks on the cover board. Be sure to hold the drill perpendicular to the board while drilling to make sure the holes are straight. Repeat this step for the remaining cover board.

6. Dust off the boards and remove your mask. Return to your normal work area.

MAKE THE SIGNATURES

7. Organize the watercolor sheets into seven stacks of three sheets each. Place one handmade paper sheet beneath each stack. Jog one of the stacks so the side and bottom edges are even. With a bone folder, fold the stack into a signature. Repeat with the remaining 6 stacks.

Optional: If you like, you can hand-letter a Materia Medica title page (page 70).

PUNCH HOLES IN THE SIGNATURES

8. Nest the folded punch guide inside each of the signatures in turn. With your awl, punch holes for each sewing station. Stack the signatures into a text block.

ASSEMBLE THE BOOK

9. Cut four 3-inch (7.6 cm) lengths from the jute cord.

10. Position the text block so the spine is facing you. Set the 3-inch (7.6 cm) lengths of jute cord near stations 2, 3, 5, and 6 of the text block. Place the remaining long cord at station 4.

11. Pull the bottom signature from the stack. Enter the threaded needle into station 1 from the outside of the signature. Draw the thread inside the signature, leaving a 12-inch (30.5 cm) tail on the outside of the signature.

12. Enter into sewing station 2 and pull the thread to the outside of the signature. Insert the needle back into the same station **(B)**. Pull the thread into the signature while leaving a small loop of thread on the outside of the cover. Place a 3-inch (7.6 cm) length of cord into the loop of station 2 **(C)**. The loop should wrap around the jute cord ¼ inch (6 mm) from the bottom end. Pull the thread taut to cinch the cord in place.

13. Repeat step 12 at the next four stations. You will cinch each loop ¼ inch (6 mm) from the bottom of the cord, except at station 4. At this station, cinch the loop at the center of the long jute cord instead.

14. After looping around the last length of jute cord and drawing the thread to the inside of the signature, draw the needle to station 7 and exit to the outside of the signature. Pull the thread taut and make sure all cords are cinched tightly.

15. Pull the next signature from the bottom of the stack and direct-link it to the previous signature by entering the needle into station 7 of the new signature. Continue sewing the signature the same way as above, but going from left to right. Make sure you loop your thread around the jute cords rather than stitching through them with the needle. Once you reach station 1, pull all threads taut and link the loose thread to the tail hanging from the first signature with a square knot.

Tip: Before adding a new signature, gently press the newly sewn one down so it rests snugly against the previously sewn one. This will help strengthen and tighten the binding.

16. Continue binding the remaining signatures with running stitches that loop around the jute cords. Link all the signatures at the end sewing stations to the previous signature's end station with a true kettle stitch (page 23). Complete the binding with a true kettle stitch at the last station **(D)**.

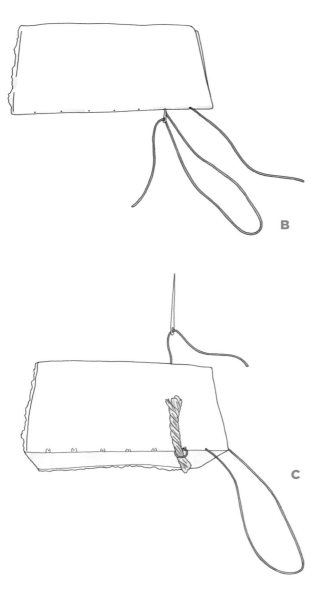

B

C

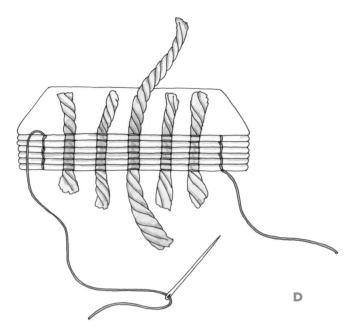

TRIM THE CORDS

18. With scissors, trim the short jute cords so the ends are flush with the edges of the cover boards. The cords will fray over time to create a beautiful, rustic texture.

19. With the remaining binder's thread, tie a knot around each end of the long jute cord. Wrap the thread tightly around the cord end about five times; then tie off the thread at the tail with a square knot. Trim the tail to $\frac{1}{16}$ inch (2 mm). Tying off the cord's ends will prevent them from fraying.

20. To secure your book, wrap the long jute cord around the cover and tie the ends together in a loose square knot. Clip a writing utensil on the cord near the fore edges of the cover for easy use while you're out and about.

D

17. Attach the covers (page 24) and tie off the loose threads (see Tying Off the Binding, page 27).

JOURNALING INSPIRATION

Take a field trip to a park or nature preserve near your neighborhood and record your observations. Identify local plants and animals using a field guide, draw your findings, and collect common specimens to press between the pages. Be sure to leave any rare species or small groups of plants so they can flourish and continue their life cycle. Make sure you also know the local laws, specifically whether you're permitted to collect any natural materials, especially in land preserves or other protected environments.

HAND-LETTERED
TITLE PAGE

Put ink to paper and let the purpose of your book be known. Add a custom title page to any, or all, of your books.

WHAT YOU NEED

1 sheet of text-weight paper, 8½ × 11 inches (21.6 × 28 cm)

Template

Scrap paper

Soft graphite pencil

Scissors

Signature or page from your book

Ruler

Fine-point pen

Eraser

1. Photocopy the template onto the text-weight paper.

2. Make a rough sketch of your lettering design on scrap paper.

3. With the ruler and pencil, mark the center points of the top and bottom edge of the page of your signature. Draw a very light, almost invisible pencil line connecting the two marks. Decide where you would like to position your type. Draw straight horizontal lines to mark where the bottoms of your letters will be placed.

MATERIA
MEDICA
————

A B C D E F G H I
J K L M N O P Q R
S T U V W X Y Z

A a B b C c D d E e
F f G g H h I i J j
K k L l M m N n O o
P p Q q R r S s T t U u
V v W w X x Y y Z z

. , ( ) & " ' - –
1 2 3 4 5 6 7 8 9 0

Template 1: 3½ × 5⅞ inches (8.9 × 15 cm)
Enlarge template 125%

4. Flip the typography template over. The blank back side will be facing up. With your pencil, scribble a solid coating of graphite over the back side of the characters you will be using. If you plan to use the same letter more than once, you can reuse the same template, but add an additional layer of graphite for each individual use. With scissors, cut out the individual letters, leaving a rectangular border around the edges.

5. To center your type, count the number of characters and spaces on one line of your design. Determine the character that is at the center of your word or phrase. Choose the matching character from the typography template. Position it onto your page, graphite-side down so the bottom of the letter aligns with the horizontal line and is centered on the vertical line. With your pencil, trace the character on the front side of your template. Use enough pressure so the graphite from the back of the guide transfers onto your signature. Continue positioning the characters on either side of the center character and transferring them onto the page.

6. Repeat step 5 for each line of your lettering design.

7. With a fine-point pen, ink over the graphite transfers to bold your letters and add high contrast to your design.

8. Once all letters are inked and dry to the touch, use an eraser to remove any faint pencil lines or marks. Return the signature to your book and continue binding as instructed.

THE WRITER

IF YOU HAVE A SERIOUS WRITING HABIT, THIS REFILLABLE JOURNAL
WILL KEEP UP WITH YOUR DEMAND FOR BLANK PAGES.

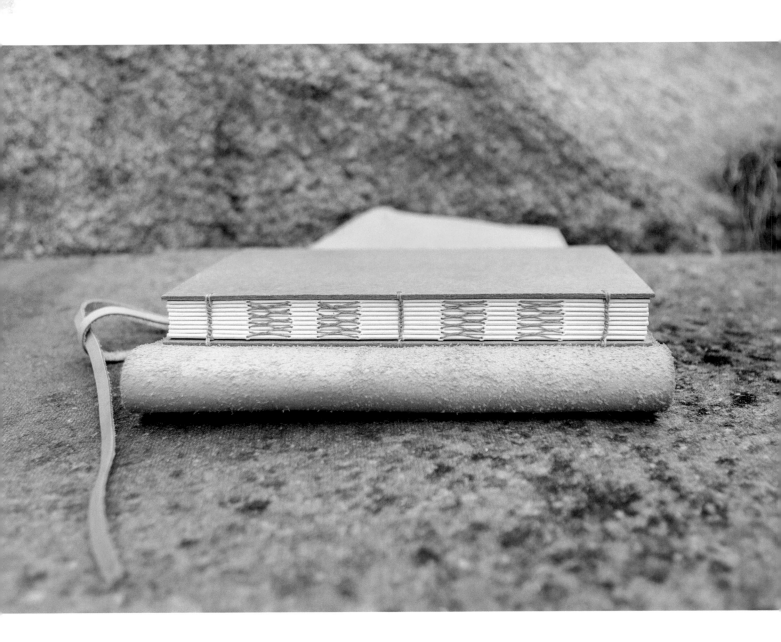

Finished Dimensions

6 × 9 × 1½ inches (15.2 × 22.9 × 3.8 cm)

Binding Techniques

Chain stitch (page 21)

French stitch (page 23)

True kettle stitch (page 23)

What You Need

Basic Bookbinding Toolkit (page 11)

Bookbinding thread, 100 inches (254 cm),
   36 inches (91.4 cm), and 12 inches (30.5 cm)

Cardstock for template

2 pieces of binder's board, 5⅝× 8⅝ inches
   (14.3 × 21.9 cm), for covers

54 sheets of text-weight paper, 8½ × 11 inches
   (21.6 × 27.9 cm)

2- to 3-ounce (0.8 mm to 1.2 mm thick) leather
   for the wraparound cover: 18 × 9 inches
   (45.7 × 22.9 cm) and 4 × 9 inches (10.2 ×
   22.9 cm)

2- to 3-ounce (0.8 mm to 1.2 mm thick) leather
   strip, ¼ × 36 inches (6 mm × 91.4 cm)

Tip: To create a beautiful raw edge along the wraparound flap of your cover, cut your leather from the edge of the hide.

MAKE THE SIGNATURES

1. Divide the text-weight paper into nine groups of six sheets. Fold each group into a signature measuring 5½ × 8½ inches (14 × 21.6 cm). Stack them into a text block.

PUNCH HOLES IN THE SIGNATURE

2. Use the cardstock to make a punch guide from Template 1. Number the stations. Nest the guide into the center of one of the signatures and use an awl to punch the sewing stations **(A)**. Repeat for the remaining signatures. Stack the signatures with the spines facing you.

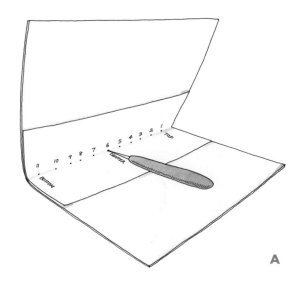

A

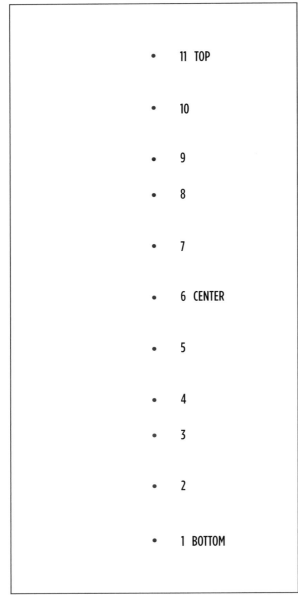

•   **11 TOP**

•   **10**

•   **9**

•   **8**

•   **7**

•   **6 CENTER**

•   **5**

•   **4**

•   **3**

•   **2**

•   **1 BOTTOM**

Template 1: Signature Punch Guide, 4 × 8½ inches
(10 × 21.6 cm). Enlarge template 125%.

3. Place the binder's board covers on your work surface. Sandwich the folded punch guide between the boards. Slide one of the cover boards ¼ inch (6 mm) away from the folded edge of the guide so that the sewing stations are visible. Make certain the guide is vertically centered within the edges of

the board. Use a pencil to mark the top, center, and bottom holes on the top cover board ⅛ inch (3 mm) away from the spine edge **(B)**. Punch only the three marked holes into the board with an awl or ³⁄₁₆ inch (5 mm) hole punch.

B

4. Place the punched board over the bottom cover board, making sure the spine edges align. Using the punched top cover board as a guide, mark the three holes onto the bottom board as for the top board. Set the top board aside and punch the marked holes into the bottom board. Align the signatures into a block, with spines facing you on the worktable. Nestle the text block between the cover boards.

ASSEMBLE THE BOOK

5. Pull the bottom cover and bottom signature (signature 1) from the text block. With a needle and the 100-inch (254 cm) piece of thread, enter station 1 from the outside of the signature. Draw the thread to the inside of the signature until there is a 12-inch (30.5 cm) tail on the outside. Enter into station 2 and pull the thread to the outside of the signature. Enter station 3 and pull the thread back inside the signature. Continue with this running stitch pattern (page 18) until your thread is on the outside of station 6, the center station of the signature.

6. Place the bottom cover board beneath your signature. To attach the cover at the center station (6) of the signature, pass the thread twice around and through the center hole of the board **(C)**. Pull the thread taut. Bring the needle back into the center hole of the signature. Continue sewing a running stitch until you are on the outside of the sewing station 11.

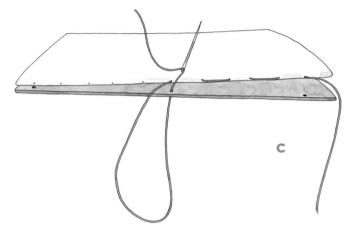

C

7. Pull the next signature (signature 2) from the bottom of the unsewn text block and place it on top of the sewn signature. Draw the needle and thread into the station 11 on the new signature **(D)**. Pull the thread to the inside of the signature and pull taut. Enter into station 10 of signature 2 and pull the thread to the outside of the signature. Link to the thread between stations 10 and 9 of the previous signature using a French stitch (page 23).

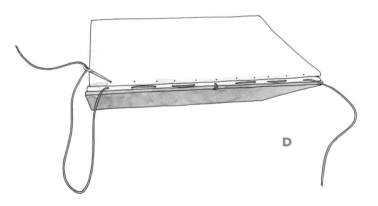

D

8. Draw the thread inside the new signature and continue to station 8. Bring the thread outside and again link to the previous signature with a French stitch between stations 8 and 7. Draw the thread to the inside the signature and continue until you reach the center station (6).

9. On the outside of the center station, link to the stitch between the previous signature and the cover with a chain stitch (page 21) **(E)**. Return the needle to the inside of the new signature at the center station. Continue sewing the next half of the signature as before, linking it to the previous signature with French stitches. Once the needle is on the outside of the top station (station 1), link to the top station of the previous signature with a true kettle stitch (page 23).

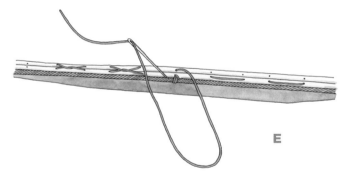

E

10. Continue attaching signatures 3 through 8 by repeating steps 7 and 9.

11. To attach the last signature, begin by linking it to the previous signature with a French stitch between stations 2 and 3, and 4 and 5. When you reach the center station (6) of the last signature, attach to the center of the remaining cover board by passing the thread twice through and around the center cover hole **(F)**. Link to the previous signature with a chain stitch; then enter the center station of the last signature. Continue linking the last signature to the previous signature with French stitches and attach the end of the signature to the end of the previous one with a true kettle stitch.

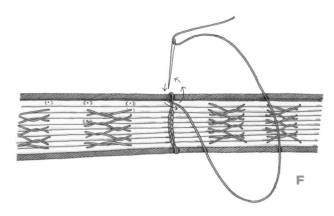

12. Beginning at the final station with the threaded needle, attach the text block to the top cover board, hike the thread down the spine to the back cover board, and then attach the back cover board (see Attaching the Covers, page 24). Tie off the threads on the inside of the nearest signature and trim the tails to ¼ inch (6 mm). Thread the needle with the tail that you left at the start of the sewing and repeat the above instructions to attach the covers on the bottom of the spine.

MAKE THE WRAPAROUND LEATHER COVER

13. Use the remaining cardstock to create a punch guide from Template 2.

14. The leather cover will feature a stitched inner flap to hold the front cover board of the refillable journal in place. Start by perforating the leather flap and wraparound cover with holes that will be stitched together. Center Template 2 on the front side of the 4 × 9–inch (10.2 × 22.9 cm) piece of leather, which will become the inside flap of the cover. Use an awl to mark the holes and to trace the two curved corners onto the leather. With a small punch, perforate the holes along the edges. Cut the curved corners using scissors.

Template 2: Cover Punch Guide, 4 × 9 inches (10.2 × 22.9 cm). Enlarge template 133%.

15. Place the large piece of leather for the cover with the back side facing your worktable and long edge parallel to the edge of your work table. Position Template 2 so that the holes are along the left edge of the leather. Use an awl to mark the holes and corner curves. With a hole punch and scissors, punch the holes and cut the curves.

16. Position the 4 × 9–inch (10.2 × 22.9 cm) piece of leather on the back of the cover, aligning the edges with the punched holes and the holes themselves. The back sides of the leather should be facing each other. Thread your needle and the 36-inch (91.4 cm) binder's thread. Starting from the back side of the 4 × 9–inch (10.2 × 22.9 cm) piece of leather, draw the needle up through the bottom right hole. Leave a 2-inch (5.1 cm) tail on the underside of the flap. Wrap the thread around the bottom edge of both the flap and the cover and enter into the bottom right hole in the cover **(G)**. Attach the thread to the tail with a square knot (page 28) and then draw the needle and thread back through the same hole in the cover. The thread will now be on the outside of the wraparound cover.

17. Guide your needle through the second hole on both pieces of leather. Pull the thread taut. Continue this step over and over to form a whipstitched edge (page 29) **(H)**.

18. Once you reach the final hole, complete one more whipstitch and then guide the needle through the top hole of the flap. Gently spread the leather pieces apart and draw the needle under the stitched thread, connecting them from the bottom side **(I)**. Form a loose square knot, pull the thread before the knot taut, then tighten the knot. Trim this tail and the first one to ¼ inch (6 mm).

19. Slip the front board of the text block into the flap of the leather cover and wrap the cover around the text block.

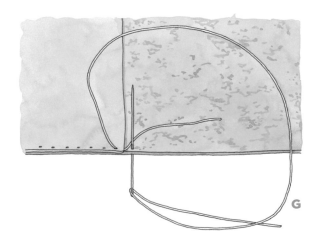

G

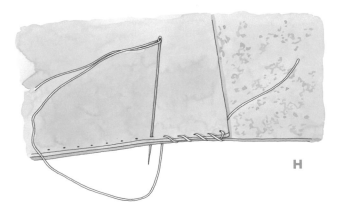

H

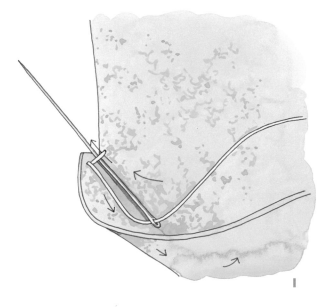

I

ATTACH THE CLOSURE

20. Take the thin leather strip and punch two holes into one end of it, approximately ¼ inch (6 mm) apart. Place this end of the leather strip on the front cover of the leather wraparound flap about ½ inch (1.3 cm) from the edge of the flap. Use an awl to mark the holes from the strap onto the leather flap. Punch the holes into the flap.

21. Open the leather cover and place one end of the strip on top of the cover, aligning the holes in the strip with the holes in the flap. The back sides of both the cover and the strip should be facing up.

22. To sew the tie to the cover, thread a needle and 12 inches (30.5 cm) of binder's thread. Starting from the inside of the cover, enter through one of the holes in the tie and pull the thread to the outside of the cover, leaving a tail of thread 2 inches (5.1 cm) long. Enter into the second hole on the cover and pull the thread to the inside of the tie. Repeat to create a second stitch between the two holes.

23. Tie off the thread on the inside of the cover to the first thread tail with a double knot **(J)**. Trim the thread ends to ¼ inch (6 mm). Wrap the tie around the book twice and tuck the end beneath the front straps to close.

REFILL YOUR JOURNAL

24. Once you've filled the pages of this journal, remove the completed book and make a new text block with covers by following steps 1 through 12. Repeat as often as needed!

JOURNALING INSPIRATION

Keep your words flowing by filling at least two to four pages each day. Approach your writing without judgment and record any thoughts, feelings, words, and phrases that come to mind without editing them. Stream-of-conscious writing can reveal what is going on in your subconscious mind. Trust that the writing that flows onto the paper is a message to your conscious self!

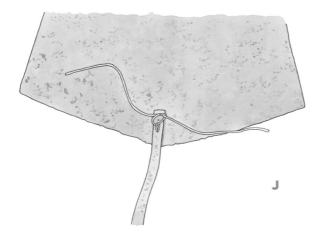

J

THE VISIONARY

THIS ONE IS FOR THE SEERS, THE BELIEVERS, AND THE MAGIC-MAKERS—
A CIRCULAR BOOK TO RECORD THE SYMBOLS, CYCLES, AND MARKS
THAT HAVE MEANING FOR YOU.

Finished Dimensions

2 ½ × 5½ × ½ inches (6.4 × 14 × 1.3 cm)

Binding Techniques

Pamphlet-stitch variation (page 18)

What You Need

Basic Bookbinding Toolkit (page 11)

Bookbinding thread in color of your choice, 36 inches (91.4 cm)

Bookbinding thread in second color of your choice, two 12-inch (30.5 cm) lengths

11 sheets of text-weight paper, 5½ × 5½ inches (14 × 14 cm)

Cardstock for template

2-ounce (0.8 mm thick) vegetable-tanned leather, 5½ × 5½ inches (14 × 14 cm)

2-ounce (0.8 mm thick) vegetable-tanned leather strip, ¼ × 16 inches (6 mm × 40.6 cm)

MAKE THE COVER

1. Create a cover and signature punch guide from Template 1 on cardstock. Cut out the guide along the outer circular line.

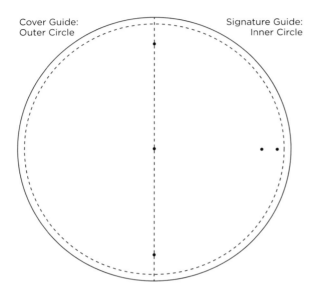

Cover Guide:
Outer Circle

Signature Guide:
Inner Circle

*Template 1: Cover and Signature Punch Guide,
5 × 5 inches (12.7 × 12.7 cm).
Enlarge template 167%.*

2. Center the guide on the front side of the square piece of leather. With a pencil, trace the circular edge of the guide onto the leather. Using an awl, mark the three sewing stations and the two other dots onto the leather. With scissors, cut the leather into a circle. Punch the five holes with a leather punch.

Optional: Decorate the outer side of the leather cover with stamping (page 83).

MAKE THE SIGNATURES

3. With scissors, cut along the dotted circle line of the guide. Fold the guide (Template 1) in half along the straight dotted line.

4. With your bone folder, fold each sheet of text-weight paper in half. Nest the folded sheets inside one another to create a single signature.

5. Remove the outer folded sheet of paper. Fold the template over the paper, making sure the folded edges align. With a pencil, trace around the rounded edge of the template onto the page. With scissors, cut out the circle from the folded sheet.

6. Remove the next folded sheet from the signature and nest it inside the first cut signature sheet. Use a pencil to trace the edge of the inner sheet onto the outer sheet. With scissors, cut the outer sheet along the pencil mark. Nest the newly cut sheet inside the first cut sheet. Repeat this step, working with one sheet of paper at a time, until all eleven sheets are cut and nested into a single circle-shaped signature.

PUNCH HOLES IN THE SIGNATURES

7. Nest the punch guide into the rounded signature. With your awl, punch the three stations along the center line.

ASSEMBLE THE BOOK

8. With your hands, gently crease the leather cover in half along the center sewing stations. Nest the signature into the cover.

9. Thread the needle with the 36-inch (91.4 cm) length of binder's thread. Enter the needle into the center sewing station in the inside of the signature **(A)**. Draw the thread to the outside of the cover until you have only a 3-inch (7.6 cm) tail on the inside of the signature.

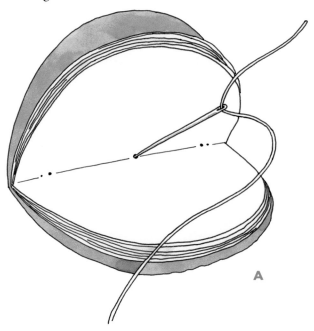

A

10. Sew the binding with a basic pamphlet stitch (page 18). Repeat the pamphlet stitch so that there are two threads running between each station. Be sure to pull the thread taut between each station.

11. Once you've reached the last station and arrived on the inside of the signature, tie off the thread to the tail using a square knot (page 28). Trim the tails to ¼ inch (6 mm).

WEAVE THE STITCHING (OPTIONAL)

12. Thread the needle with the 12-inch (30.5 cm) length of thread. Open the book to the center signature. Anchor the long end of the thread to the thread near an end sewing station (page 29). Enter

the needle through that sewing station and draw the thread to the outside of the cover. Pull the thread taut.

13. Orient the book with the outside facing up, and the pamphlet stitches running vertically.

Tip: If you are seated, hold the journal between your knees to free your hands.

14. Weave over and under each individual thread on the binding **(B)**. Guide the needle under the left pamphlet stitch thread and draw the needle to the left until it is taut. Guide the needle to the center of the threads, pointing the needle under the right thread. Draw the needle to the right around the right thread and pull taut. Continue weaving from left to right to create a decorative pattern. Once you reach the center sewing station, continue weaving down over the center sewing station toward the bottom station. When you've reached the sewing station on the opposite end from where you started, enter into that station. Pull the thread to the inside of the signature and tie off the binding to the thread nearby. Trim tails to ¼ inch (6 mm).

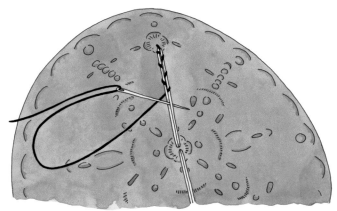

B

ATTACH THE TIE

15. Position one end of the leather strip under the two holes on the cover. Using your awl, mark the position of the holes onto the end of the strip **(C)**. It will become the book's tie. Punch the marked holes with the leather punch.

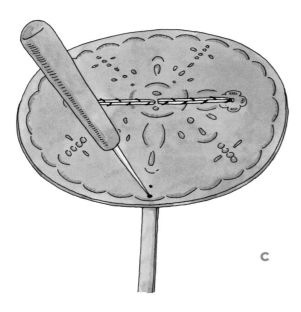

C

16. With a needle and 12 inches (30.5 cm) of binder's thread, sew the tie to the cover, placing the tie end inside the cover and starting to stitch on the inside of the cover. To do this, enter through one of the holes in the tie and pull the thread to the outside of the cover, leaving a tail of thread inside. Enter into the second hole on the cover and pull the thread to the inside of the tie. Repeat.

17. Tie off the thread on the inside of the cover to the first thread tail with a double knot. Trim the thread ends to ¼ inch (6 mm).

18. To close the book, wrap the tie around the bound book twice, and secure it by tucking the loose end beneath the wrapped tie.

JOURNALING INSPIRATION

Explore the symbols in your life. Which ones have shown up for you, and what do they signify? Do they hold personal significance for you?

LEATHER STAMPING

Add decorative elements to your leather journal with this analog stamping technique. Consider sketching out your design prior to stamping, or create your design as you go!

WHAT YOU NEED

2- to 4-ounce (0.8 to 1.6 mm thick) vegetable-tanned leather cover

Scrap leather for practice and cushioning, the same size as your cover

A variety of metal hand-stamping tools

Rubber mallet

Sponge or absorbent cloth

Water

Note: This type of stamping won't work on oil-stained leathers because the oil content makes the leather supple, thus preventing you from making a clearly defined impression. Make sure your leather is vegetable-tanned.

1. Place the leather cover front-side up on your work surface.

2. Use a wet sponge or cloth to saturate the surface of the leather cover with water. Let the leather sit for a minute to fully absorb the water.

3. Position the tip of your metal stamping tool onto the leather, holding the stamp at a 90° angle to the work surface. Using your mallet, firmly tap the end of the tool two to four times. You may wish to practice on a scrap piece of leather beforehand. Continue using your tools and mallet in this way until you've finished your design.

Tip: Place a piece of scrap leather beneath the leather cover to make a deeper impression. The extra padding beneath the leather will allow the stamp to penetrate more deeply into the surface.

THE FREE FOLK

THIS LIGHTWEIGHT, ECO-FRIENDLY BOOK IS FOR NATURALISTS,
FLOWER CHILDREN, AND LOVERS OF EARTH—PERFECT FOR TOTING
ALONG ON YOUR OUTDOOR ADVENTURES.

Finished Dimensions

7¼ × 4½ × 1 inches (18.4 × 11.4 × 2.5 cm)

Binding Technique

Long-stitch variation (page 19)

What You Need

Basic Bookbinding Toolkit (page 11)

Bookbinding thread, 85 inches (215.9 cm), 12 inches (30.5 cm)

15 sheets of handmade cotton rag paper with deckle edges, 8 × 7 inches (20.3 × 17.9 cm)

2 sheets of decorative handmade paper, 4¾ × 7 inches (12 × 18 cm)

Cardstock for templates

2- to 4-ounce (0.8 to 1.6 mm thick) buckskin leather: 12 × 7½ inches (30.5 × 19.1 cm) for cover

Two lengths of ¾-inch (6 mm) wide strip of 2- to 4-ounce (0.4 to 1.2 mm thick) stoned-oil or veg-tanned leather, each 29 inches (6 mm × 73.7 cm) long for strap

⅜-inch (1 cm) wide 2- to 4-ounce (0.4 to 1.2 mm thick) strip of leather, 36 inches (91.4 cm) long for tie

Tip: Go green by using your scrap leather or old leather belts for the straps. In lieu of leather, try recyclable synthetic leathers or non-leather alternatives, such as thick canvas and oilcloth.

Template 1: Signature Punch Guide, 3 × 7 inches (7.6 × 17.8 cm). Shown at full size.

STRAP B		STRAP A		1
				2
				3
				4
				5

Template 2: Strap Punch Guide, ¾ × 8½ inches (1.9 × 21.6 cm). Shown at full size.

MAKE THE COVER

1. Create cardstock punch guides using Templates 1 and 2.

2. Place the 12 × 7½ inch (30.5 × 19.1 cm) rectangular piece of leather horizontally on your worktable with the back side facing up. Vertically center Template 2 and place it 4 inches (10.2 cm) from the left edge on the back side of the leather. Use a pen to mark the all the holes for sewing stations 2 and 3 onto the leather. Using a leather hole punch, punch the ten sewing stations into the leather. Roll the leather from the edge to reach the holes with the punch.

3. Place the two 36-inch (91.4 cm) long straps on your work surface so both ends meet. Center Template 2 on top of the straps so the ends meet along the dashed line **(A)**. Use a pen to mark all holes onto the leather straps. Each strap should have 10 hole marks. Set the template aside and use a leather punch to make holes in the straps.

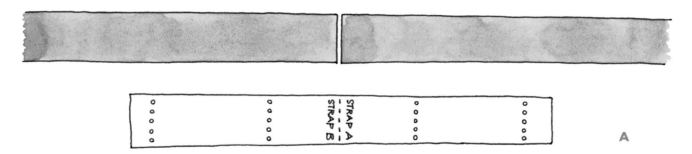

A

MAKE THE SIGNATURES

4. Divide the sheets into five stacks of 3 sheets each. Fold each stack into a signature measuring 4 × 7 inches (10.2 × 17.9 cm). Arrange the folded signatures into a text block.

5. Wrap one of the decorative sheets around the top signature. Align one edge of the decorative end sheet with the fore edge of the signature and wrap the excess paper around the fold of the signature. Repeat for the bottom signature.

PUNCH HOLES IN THE SIGNATURES

6. Nest the signature punch guide into a signature and use your awl to punch the two stations along the center line. Repeat for all remaining signatures. Arrange the signatures into a text block.

ASSEMBLE THE BOOK

7. Position the leather cover vertically on your worktable with the back side of the leather facing up and the fore edge towards you. Align the sewing stations on the spine straps, back sides facing up, with the sewing stations on the cover **(B)**. Position the text block with the spines facing you.

8. Pull the bottom signature from the text block and align sewing stations 2 and 3 with the sewing stations in row 1 of the strap. Lift the fore edge of the cover with one hand. With the needle threaded with 85 inches (215.9 cm) of binder's thread in the other, enter the needle into station 2, row 1 of the cover from the outside of the cover. Draw the needle through the cover and station 2, row 1 of the strap, and into the center of the signature, leaving a tail of 10 inches (25.4 cm) on the outside of the cover

9. Draw the needle into station 3 from the inside of the signature and pull the thread back to the outside of the cover. Move the needle into station 4 in the strap. Pull the thread through the strap until it is taut. Enter into station 3 from the inside of the same signature and pull through the spine and to the outside of the cover.

10. Pull the next signature from the bottom of the text block and direct-link it to the previous one by entering the needle into row 2, station 3 of the cover **(C)**. Draw the needle into station 4 of the strap and towards the outside of the cover and then back into the inside of the second signature at station 3. At station 2, pull the thread through to the outside of the cover. Enter into station 1 on the strap, drawing the thread to the inside of the signature and pulling taut. Enter into station 2 in the same signature and pull the thread to the outside of the cover.

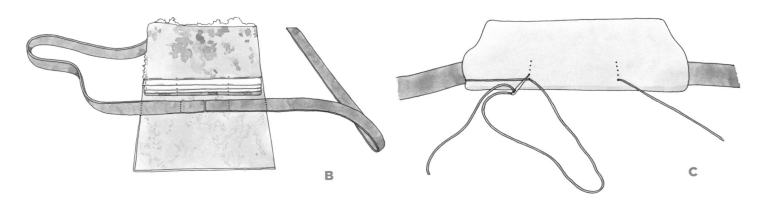

B

C

11. Continue sewing the remaining signatures in this pattern.

12. When your final signature is fully sewn, pull the thread into the inside of the signature at row 4, station 2. Tie off to the nearest thread (page 27). Trim ends to ¼ inch (6 mm).

13. Thread the needle onto the tail you left at the beginning of the binding. Starting from the outside of the cover, draw the needle into station 1 of the strap. Enter into station 2 from the inside of the signature. Pull the thread to the outside of the cover and draw up into row 2, station 2 to the inside of the signature. Tie off to the nearest thread (page 27). Trim ends to ¼ inch (6 mm).

ATTACH THE TIE

14. Use a pen to mark five holes ⅛ inch (3 mm) apart and ½ inch (1.3 cm) from the edge of the diagonal cover flap to attach the tie. Punch the holes with a leather hole punch. Align one end of the ⅜-inch (1 cm) wide tie underneath the cover holes. Use a pen to mark the points on the tie and use a hole punch to make the holes.

15. Position the tie on the inside of the cover so the holes align and the back side of the tie is facing down. This will make the suede side of the strap visible when you wrap it around the cover. With 12 inches (30.5 cm) of thread and a needle, enter into the hole nearest the spine and draw the thread through the hole of the strap to the outside of the cover. Continue sewing the tie to the cover by moving your needle in and out of the five holes until all spaces between holes have been stitched. Tie the ends off on the inside of the cover and trim thread ends to ⅛ inch (3 mm) **(D)**.

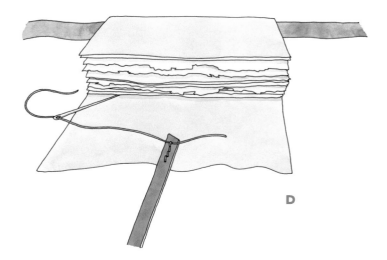

D

16. Align the loose ends of the straps so that they are even and the back side of the ends are facing up. Pressing the ends together, tie them together with a loop knot (page 28). Your journal is ready to go.

Optional: Add a pine needle bookmark (page 89).

PINE NEEDLE BOOKMARK

Never lose your place with this playful, tassel-inspired bookmark.

FINISHED DIMENSIONS

¼ × 7½ × ¼ inches (6 mm × 19 cm × 6 mm)

KNOTS USED

Whip knot (page 29)

Square knot (page 28)

WHAT YOU NEED

1 pine needle branch

Bookbinding thread, 28 inches (71 cm)

Binder's needle

Note: If you are harvesting from trees in a city or in a park, be sure to request permission from the trees' caretakers before doing so!

1. Pine needles naturally grow in clusters. Pull five to seven clusters of pine needles from the branch. Gather them into a small bundle with the branch ends grouped at one end.

2. Hold the bundle in one hand. With the other, form a small loop with the longer end of the thread, leaving a 10-inch (25 cm) tail.

3. Tie the handle with a whip knot (page 29). Hold the loop against the bundle of pine needle clusters with your thumb. Wrap the thread tightly around the bundle and around the bottom of the loop seven times. Pass the end of the wrapped thread through the loop. Cinch the loop closed by pulling the 10-inch (25 cm) tail upward and away from the bundle. The loop will be drawn and secured beneath the wrapped thread.

4. Using scissors, trim the thread tail so that it is no longer visible. If needed, trim the rough knobs of the needles to make them smoother.

5. To attach the bookmark to a journal, thread the long end of the thread with a needle. Place the journal in an upright position; the top of the spine should be facing up. Draw the needle beneath one of the stitches between the spine and the signatures. Adjust the height of the pine bookmark by pulling the thread through the stitch. Tie off the ends near the spine with a square knot (page 28) and trim them to ⅛ inch (3 mm).

Tip: Try using a feather, cedar bough, dried wheat stalks, reeds, or other botanical materials to make your next bookmark. Simply bundle the materials together, if needed, and then follow steps 2 through 6.

THE MYSTIC

GROUND YOUR ILLUMINATING AND EXTRAORDINARY EXPERIENCES IN EVERYDAY REALITY WITHIN THESE TASSELED COVERS.

Finished Dimensions

4¼ × 8 × ¼ inches (10.8 × 20.3 × 1.9 cm)

Binding Techniques

Long-stitch variation (page 19) with French stitches (page 23)

What You Need

Basic Bookbinding Toolkit (page 11)

Bookbinding thread in color of your choice: one 20-inch (50.8 cm) length for the binding, one 10-inch (25.4 cm) length for the cover flap, one 40-inch (102 cm) length for the tasseled tie, and two 42-inch (107 cm) lengths for the tassels on the spine

Bookbinding thread in second color of your choice: one 20-inch (50.8 cm) length for the binding, one 10-inch (25.4 cm) length for the cover flap, one 40-inch (102 cm) length for the tassel tie, four 12-inch (30.5 cm) lengths for the tassels on the spine

40 sheets text-weight paper, 8 × 7½ inches (20.3 × 19 cm)

2 sheets of decorative paper, 4¾ × 7½ inches (12 × 19 cm)

Cardstock for templates

Upholstery fabric for cover, 13 × 8 inches (33 × 20.3 cm)

3- to 4-ounce (1.2 to 1.6 mm thick) leather or binder's board, ½ × 7½ inches (1.3 × 19 cm)

Binder's clamp or paper clip

MAKE THE SIGNATURES

1. Divide the text-weight sheets into groups of five sheets each. Using a bone folder, fold each group into a signature measuring 4 × 7½ inches (10.2 × 19 cm) to make a total of eight signatures.

2. Double the thickness of the signatures by nesting one signature inside another. You'll now have a total of four thick signatures.

3. Place a decorative paper on the top page of the first signature (signature 1) and after the last page of the final signature (signature 4). Wrap the extra width of the decorative papers around the spines of their respective signatures **(A)**.

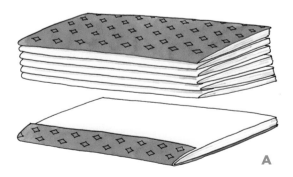

A

PUNCH HOLES IN THE SIGNATURES

4. Make a signature punch guide on cardstock from Template 1. Nest the guide into the center of each signature. With an awl, punch the sewing stations.

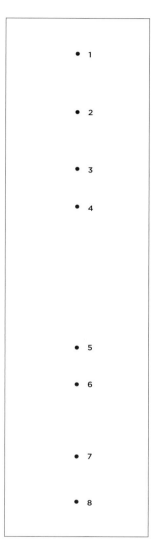

Template 1: Signature Punch Guide, 2 × 7½ inches (5 × 19 cm). Enlarge template 133%.

5. Stack all the signatures in the order they will appear when bound.

									1
									2
									3
									4 ROW

Template 2: Spine Punch Guide, ½ × 7½ inches (1.3 × 19 cm). Shown at full size.

ASSEMBLE THE COVER

6. Create a cover punch guide on cardstock from Template 2. Center the guide on top of the ½ × 7½–inch (1.3 × 19.2 cm) leather strip, aligning all the edges. With an awl, mark each row of sewing stations onto the leather strip. It will become the inner part of the spine of the book. Punch the holes into the leather using a punch.

7. Position the upholstery fabric horizontally on your worktable with the back side facing up and the long edge facing you. Using a ruler, measure 4 inches (10.2 cm) from the left edge of the fabric and, with a pencil, make marks near the top and bottom edges. Draw a straight line connecting the marks.

8. With a glue brush, lightly coat the back of the leather spine with paper glue. Holding the leather spine vertically, align the left edge of the spine along the right side of the pencil line on the cover. Lightly press the spine to adhere it to the inside of the cover.

ASSEMBLE THE BOOK

9. Pull the bottom two signatures (signatures 3 and 4) from your text block and place them inside the cover with all the sewing stations on the signatures and the spine piece aligned **(B)**. The spine should be facing you. Fold the 4-inch (10 cm) wide cover over the text block so the cloth outside of the spine is visible. You will bind two signatures at a time into the cover.

10. Thread your needle with one of the 20-inch (50.8 cm) threads. Locate the position of the bottom right sewing station (station 1, row 4) on the cover. You may need to press the needle through the sewing station on the inside of the leather spine piece out

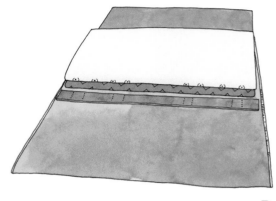

B

through the cover to locate the sewing station on the outside of the cloth spine.

11. Begin sewing signatures 3 and 4: Enter the thread through the cover and into sewing station 1 of signature 4. Draw the thread into the signature, leaving a 4-inch (10.2 cm) tail on the outside of the cover. Insert the needle into station 2 and pull it through to the outside of the cover. Move the needle up to row 3 and into sewing station 3 of the cover. Draw the thread through and enter into station 3 of the third signature. Enter into station 4 of the third signature and draw the thread to the outside of the cover again. Enter into sewing station 5 in row 4 of the cover and pull the thread to the inside of the fourth signature **(C)**. Enter into station 6 and pull the thread back to the outside of the cover. Pull the thread taut.

12. Continue sewing signature 3: Enter the needle into station 7 in row 3 and pull the thread inside the third signature. Draw the needle through station 8, row 3, and to the outside of the cover. Pull all threads taut. Then enter the needle into station 8, row 4, and pull the thread through to the inside of signature 4.

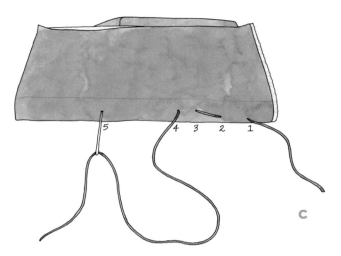

C

13. Draw the needle to the right and into station 7 in row 4 of signature 4 and pull the thread back to the outside of the cover.

14. Make a French stitch by wrapping your thread three times around the running stitch between stations 7 and 6 in row 3 **(D)**. Enter into station 6 in row 3. Continue to station 5 to the outside of the cover. At station 5, make another French stitch, this time wrapping the thread five times around the running stitch between sewing stations 4 and 5 in row 4. Enter into station 5 in row 4. Continue to station 3, row 4, to the outside of the cover. At station 3, make a third French stitch by wrapping your thread three times around the running stitch between stations 2 and 3.

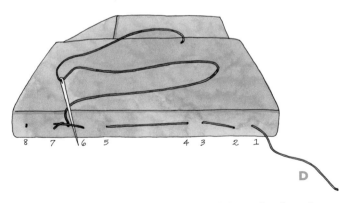

D

15. Enter into station 2 in row 3 and draw the thread to the inside. Pull the thread taut. Remove the needle. Leave the tail of the thread loose for now. It will be tied off in the next step.

16. Thread the needle onto the tail hanging from row 1, station 1. Enter the thread into station 2 in row 2. Draw the thread to the inside of the signature and tie it off to the end of the other loose thread using a square knot. Trim the ends to ¼ inch (6 mm). Thread the needle with the other 20-inch (50.8 cm) thread. Repeat steps 11–15 to bind in the remaining two signatures, but using the stations on rows 1 and 2 of the spine.

SEW THE COVER FLAP

17. To shape the triangular cover flap, open the wraparound cover of the book and orient the book so the back side of the wraparound cover faces you. Fold the two corners of the flap toward the text block to make a triangular shape. Press folds into the fabric using your fingertips.

18. Thread your needle with one of the 10-inch (25.4 cm) threads, allowing for a 2-inch (5.1 cm) tail in the needle. Tie a square knot at the end of the long length of thread.

19. Enter the needle into the back of the cover at the inside corner of the folded triangle flap, ¼ inch (6 mm) inside the edge of the fabric **(E)**. Pull the needle to the outside of the cover until the knot rests firmly against the inside of the cover.

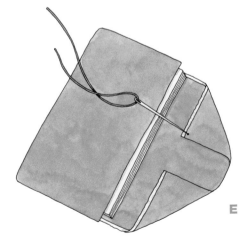

E

20. To attach the folded triangle flap to the cover, sew a series of running stitches (page 18) in a straight line about 2½ inches (6.4 cm) long. End your last stitch on the inside of the cover beneath the flap so it is hidden. Tie off the loose thread to the nearest stitch with a square knot. Trim both tails of the running stitch to ⅛ inch (3 mm).

21. Repeat steps 18–20 to sew the other triangle flap to the cover.

ATTACH THE TIE

22. Position the cover flap and turn it so the point is facing you.

23. Make a tassel (page 96) using one of the 40-inch (102 cm) threads for the attachment tie.

24. Thread a needle with the other 40-inch (102 cm) thread. Draw it through the top end of the tassel. Pull it through halfway so you have 20 inches (50.8 cm) of thread hanging from each end of the top end of the tassel. You should have a total of four 20-inch (50.8 cm) threads hanging from the tassel top.

25. Divide the threads into two groups. Place the tassel in a binder clip or a heavy book to secure it. Hold both sets of threads apart from one another and simultaneously begin to twist threads clockwise. As the threads become twisted, begin to wrap them around each other in a counterclockwise direction. This continuous motion will twine the threads together. Continue twining until 4 inches (10.2 cm) of the threads remain. Secure the twining with another binder clip or paperclip so it doesn't unwind.

26. Thread one of the ends of the twining thread onto a needle. Allow for a ½ inch (1.3 cm) tail.

27. Enter the needle into the inside of the cover ¼ inch (6 mm) from the point of the cover flap, and sew a series of running stitches (page 18) in a straight line about 1-inch (2.5 cm) long; the stitches should be about ⅛ inch (3 mm) apart from each other **(F)**. End your last stitch on the inside of the cover and pull the needle off the thread. Leave the tail of the thread loose. It will be tied off when all the lines of running stitches are complete.

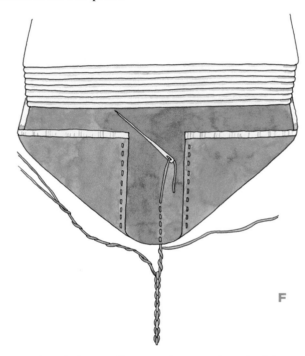

F

28. Thread the needle onto the next thread of the twined tie and make another line of running stitches, ¼ inch (6 mm) away from the previous one. Remove the needle from the thread. Repeat steps 27–28 for the two remaining threads, positioning them ¼ inch (6 mm) on the other side of the cover flap

29. Set the binder's clamp or paper clip aside. Pull at the ends of the threads so the twining cord is nestled against the edge of the triangular point of the cover.

30. Tie the first and second tails of thread from the running stitches together using a square knot. Do the same for the third and fourth tails. Trim all the ends to ½ inch (1.3 cm) **(G)**.

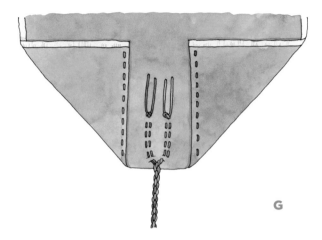

G

31. Close your book and wrap the twined tie around it once. Secure the end of the twined tie by tucking the tassel beneath the twined tie near the spine.

ATTACH THE TASSELS TO THE SPINE

32. Make two additional tassels using a 42-inch (107 cm) length of thread and two 12-inch (30.5 cm) lengths for each one (page 96).

33. Thread the needle using one of the long threads hanging from one of the tassels. Draw the needle into station 8 in row 3 at the top end of the spine on the outside of the book. Pull the thread into the inside of the nearest signature until the tassel is nestled onto the spine of the book. Repeat this process for the second long thread of the tassel. Tie the threads off onto the thread on the inside of the signature using a square knot (page 28). Trim the thread ends to ¼ inch (6 mm). Repeat this step to sew the remaining tassel onto station 1 in row 3.

JOURNALING INSPIRATION

Have you ever experienced extraordinary states of being from everyday experiences, such as prolonged periods of exercise, meditation, or time spent in nature? Use this book to record your experiences and the ways in which you perceived the world around you during those moments. Were your senses heightened? What was the catalyst for your experience? Did you receive any insights? Record any poems, invocations, or mantras that helped you along the way.

BINDER'S THREAD TASSEL

Turn your book into an ornamental beauty with this DIY tassel.

FINISHED DIMENSIONS

2 inches (5.1 cm) long

WHAT YOU NEED

3 pieces of bookbinding thread in colors of your choice: one 42-inch (107.7 cm) length, and two 12-inch (30.5 cm) length

1 piece of cardboard, 2 × 2 inches (5.1 × 5.1 cm)

Needle

Scissors

1. Wrap the 42-inch (107.7 cm) piece of thread around the cardboard twenty times.

2. Thread your needle with one of the 12-inch (30.5 cm) pieces of thread and slide the needle underneath the top of the bundle of thread. Remove the needle and pull the ends of the thread so that the center point of the 12-inch (30.5 cm) thread is beneath the bundle of wrapped thread. Tie the bundle together tightly with the 12-inch (30.5 cm) thread and secure with a square knot **(A)**. Leave the tails long.

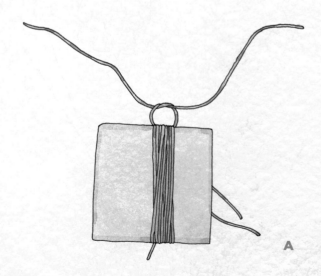

A

3. Carefully slide the bundle of thread from the cardboard. Cut the bottom loops of the bundle apart.

4. Thread your needle with the remaining 12-inch (30.5 cm) piece of thread. Hold the loose ends of the tassel along with a 3-inch (7.6 cm) tail of the 12-inch (30.5 cm) thread. With your free hand, wrap the loose end of the thread 10 times evenly around tassel, ¼ inch (6 mm) from the tassel's top **(B)**. Tie the two tails of the wrapping thread together with a square knot. To hide the tail ends, thread them onto a needle and push your needle through the top side of the wrapped thread to pull the ends inside the tassel. Trim off excess of wrapped 12-inch (30.5 cm) thread, but leave the thread ends the tassel is hanging from long. Trim the tassel ends evenly.

5. Attach the tassel to your book as a hanging exterior ornament by threading one of the loose ends of the thread at the top of the tassel with a needle and guiding it through a cover hole and into a signature. Repeat this process with the second loose thread at the top of the tassel. Attach the loose ends to the stitching thread inside the signature using a square knot (page 28). Trim ends to ¼ inch (6 mm). To use your tassel as a bookmark, attach the tassel in the same way as the Pine Needle Bookmark (page 89).

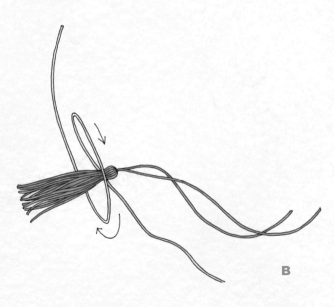

B

THE POET

COME SONG LYRIC, PROSE, OR POEM, THIS LIGHTWEIGHT BOOK IS FOR
KEEPING YOUR INSPIRATION WHEREVER IT MAY FIND YOU.

Finished Dimensions

3¼ × 8¼ × ½ inches (8.3 × 21 × 1.3 cm)

Binding Technique

Stab-binding variation, instructions below

What You Need

Basic Bookbinding Toolkit (page 11)

Bookbinding thread: one 10-inch (25.4 cm)
length, one 12-inch (30.5) length, and three
18-inch lengths (45.7 cm)

45 sheets of text-weight paper, 3 × 8 inches
(7.6 × 20.3 cm)

2 sheets of decorative paper, 3 × 8 inches
(7.6 × 20.3 cm)

Cardstock for template

2-ounce (0.8 mm thick) leather: 3¼ × 19 inches
(8.3 × 48.3 cm) for cover,
1 × 1½ inches (2.5 × 3.8 cm) for button

⅛-inch (3 mm) thick leather cord or 2-ounce
(0.8 mm thick) leather strip, 16 inches
(40.6 cm) long

MAKE THE TEXT BLOCK

1. Stack all 45 sheets of text-weight paper into a single
text block. Place a decorative sheet on the top and
bottom of the text block with the decorative sides
facing outward.

PUNCH HOLES IN THE SIGNATURES

2. Create a punch guide on cardstock using Template 1.

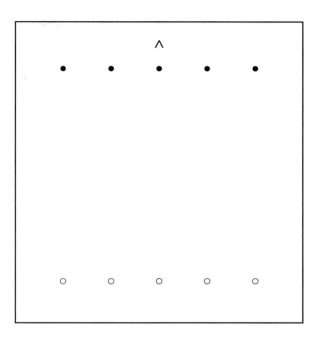

Template 1: Signature and Cover Punch Guide,
3 × 3¼ inches (7.6 × 8.3 cm). Shown at full size.

3. Position your text block so one of the short edges is
facing you. Pull the top sheet from the text block and
position the edge of the punch guide with the arrow
pointing towards the top of the sheet over it. Using
a 4 mm leather punch or paper punch, punch the
black marks of the guide onto the sheet. Lay the sheet
facedown beside the text block. Punch each sheet in
the text block in the same way. To save time, you can
punch two to four sheets at a time.

MAKE THE COVER

4. Position the large piece of leather with the front
side facing up and the short edge facing you. Pull
the top punched sheet from the text block. Align
the bottom edges of the sheet and leather cover and

center the sheet between the left and right edges of the leather. With a pencil, mark the holes of the sheet onto the leather **(A)**. Punch the marked holes.

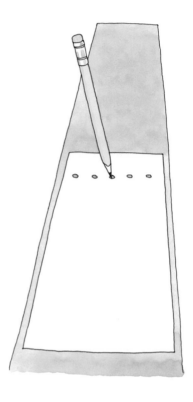

A

5. Position the template on top of the cover so the holes in the cover align with the punched holes in the template. The arrow should be pointing towards one of the shorter edges of the front cover. With an awl, mark the outlined holes onto the leather. Punch the marked holes into the leather.

ASSEMBLE THE BOOK

6. Turn over the leather cover so the back side is facing up and position it with one long edge closest to you. Place the text block inside the cover. Fold the top edge of the cover over the top of the text block. Adjust the position of the text block with the cover closed to ensure the holes align on the front and back of the text block **(B)**.

B

7. Fold the front cover over the text block. Tie a figure-eight knot (page 28) 1 inch (2.5 cm) from one end of the leather cord. Insert the loose end of the cord into the top right sewing station of the front cover and pull it to the outside of the back cover. Pull the cord until the knot on the front rests snugly against the front cover.

8. Draw the cord around the top of the spine to the next open sewing station on the front cover. Enter the cord into the station and draw it to the outside of the back cover. Continue binding around the edge until all stations have been bound and the cord end is at the back of the cover at the final station **(C)**.

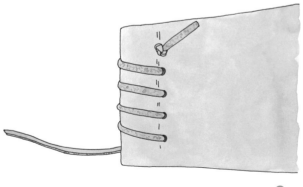

C

9. If needed, tighten the binding by pulling any loose loops of cord forward at each station. Secure the binding by tying a figure-eight knot in the cord at the back cover near the final station. Trim the end of the cord to 1 inch (2.5 cm).

MAKE THE BUTTON AND ATTACH THE CLOSURE

10. To make the leather button, position the smaller piece of leather horizontally on your work surface with the back side facing up. Fold the right edge toward the center of the leather approximately one-third of the way over. Hold the fold with your right index finger. Pick up the left edge and fold it over the top of the folded right edge. Grasping the folds in place, flip the piece over.

11. Use your awl to mark horizontal points ¼ inch (6 mm) apart in the center of the button. Then, with a firm hold on the button so it does not loosen, carefully punch each mark through all three layers of leather, using your awl.

12. Continue to hold the button together and position it at the center of the back cover flap about ¾ inch (1.9 cm) away from the cut edge. Press your awl into each of the holes in the button and mark the cover flap for button placement.

13. Open the cover flap so the back side is facing up. With a needle and 12 inches (30.5 cm) of binder's thread, sew the button to the outside of the cover flap, starting on the inside of the cover. Enter through one of the holes in the cover and pull the thread to the outside of the button. Enter into the second hole on the button and pull the thread through to the inside of the cover **(D)**. Repeat once to create two stitches between the holes. Tie off the thread on the inside of the cover with a double knot. Trim the thread ends to ¼ inch (6 mm).

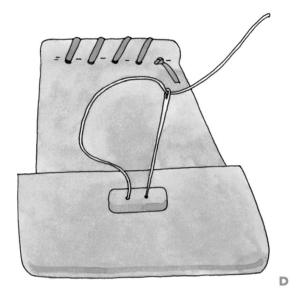

D

14. Wrap the cover flap around the book and press down on the button so the cover is in a firmly closed position. With your awl, mark one hole on the front cover of the book about ¼ inch (6 mm) above the edge of the wraparound flap and in line with the right buttonhole. Make another mark ¼ inch (6 mm) directly above the first one. Punch through the marks with your awl.

15. Group the three 18-inch (45.7 cm) threads together. Enter the ends of the threads through the top hole in the front cover. Thread the group of threads onto a needle if they do not easily slip through the holes. Pull the threads through to the inside of the cover, leaving a 3-inch (7.6 cm) tail. Enter the threads into the second hole and draw them back to the outside of the cover. Pull the threads through halfway so the strands are of equal length.

16. Divide the threads into two groups of three. Hold both sets of threads apart from one another and simultaneously begin to twist threads clockwise. As the threads become twisted, begin to wrap them around each other in a counterclockwise direction.

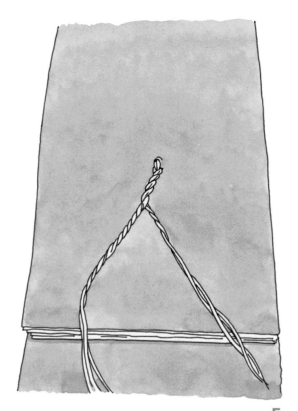

E

This continuous motion will twine the threads together **(E)**. Continue twining until 1 inch (2.5 cm) of the threads remain. Finish with an overhand knot (page 28) and trim the ends to ¼ inch (6 mm).

17. To close the book, fold the cover flap over the bottom of the book and wrap the twined thread around the leather button in a clockwise direction.

THE ALCHEMIST

USE THIS BOOK TO RECORD MOMENTS OF SELF-DISCOVERY,
KEEP YOUR ELEMENTAL RECIPES, AND MAKE SENSE OF YOUR
TRANSFORMATIVE LIFE EXPERIENCES.

Finished Dimensions

4 × 8½ × 2 inches (10.2 × 21.6 × 5.1 cm)

Binding Techniques

Long-stitch variation
(page 19)

What You Need

Basic Bookbinding Toolkit (page 11)

Metallic gold thread: 54 inches (137.2 cm) and
12 inches (30.5 cm)*

56 sheets of text-weight paper, 16 × 4 inches
(40.6 × 10.2 cm)

2 sheets of marbled paper, 9 × 4 inches
(22.9 × 10.2 cm)

Cardstock for templates

2- to 3-ounce (0.8 mm to 1.2 mm thick) leather:
20 × 11½ inches (50.8 × 29.2 cm) for cover,
¼-inch (6 mm) wide leather strap, 28 inches
(71 cm) long

Note: Depending on the type of metallic thread
you are using, you may need to double up the
thread to make it stronger. Simply thread two
single lengths of thread on the same needle
to increase the thickness and durability of the
binding.

MAKE THE TEXT BLOCK

1. Divide the text-weight papers into 7 groups of eight
sheets each.

2. Using a bone folder, fold the groups into signatures
measuring 8 × 4 inches (20.3 ×10.2 cm). You will have
a total of 7 signatures. Stack them into a text block.

3. Wrap the sheets of marbled paper around the
spines of the front and back signatures, aligning the
sheets at the fore edge and folding excess marbled
paper around the spine of their respective signatures.

PUNCH HOLES IN THE SIGNATURES

4. Make a signature punch guide from Template 1
on the cardstock. Fold the template in half so the hole
marks align on the fold. Nest the guide into the center
of each signature and use an awl to punch the holes.
Stack the signatures into a text block.

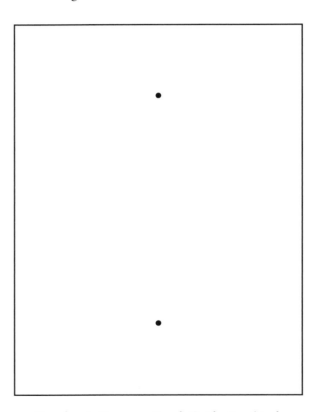

*Template 1: Signature Punch Guide, 3 × 4 inches
(7.6 × 10.2 cm). Shown at full size.*

MAKE THE COVER

5. Make a cover guide from Template 2 on cardstock.
Cut out the cover shape and preserve any markings.

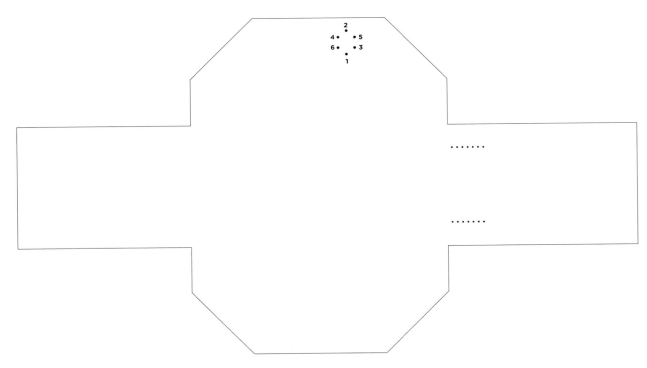

Template 2: Cover Outline and Punch Guide, 19⅝ × 11 inches (49.8 × 28 cm). Enlarge template 300%.

Template 3: Sewing Guide (for attaching text block to cover flap). Not actual size—for reference only.

6. Center the guide on top of the large piece of leather. With an awl, trace the outer edges of the guide onto the front side of the leather. Mark all holes in the guide onto the leather.

7. With scissors, cut out the leather cover using the outline from the awl as a guide. Use a leather punch to punch all the holes.

ASSEMBLE THE BOOK

8. Orient the cover with the back side facing up and the fore edge of the longer rectangular flap with the holes toward you. Place the text block nearby with spines facing you. You will begin sewing your book by referencing Template 3, the sewing guide with station and row numbers.

9. Pull the bottom signature from the text block and align the sewing stations on the signature with the ones in row 1 on the cover flap **(A)**.

A

10. Thread a needle with 54 inches (137.2 cm) of metallic gold thread. Open the signature and enter the needle into station 1. Pull the thread to the outside of the cover in row 1, station 1, leaving a 6-inch (15.2 cm) tail on the inside of the signature. Make a diagonal running stitch on the outside of the cover to station 2 of row 2.

11. Pull the next signature from the text block and direct-link it to the previous one by entering the needle into station 2 in row 2 of the new signature. Draw the needle into station 1 of signature 2. Pull the thread taut after you've entered into each station.

12. Continue adding signatures and sewing in this diagonal pattern of running stitches until your needle is in the inside of the final signature.

13. Draw the needle into station 1 in the seventh signature and pull it through to the outside of the cover. Pull on all the threads on the outside of the cover to make sure the binding is taut.

14. To complete the binding, enter the needle into station 2 in row 1 of the cover, making a long downward diagonal stitch, and pull the thread through to the inside of the first signature. Again, pull all threads taut. Tie off the thread to the tail on the inside using a square knot (page 28). Trim the tails to ½ inch (1.3 cm).

ATTACH THE TIE

15. Open the cover flap with the six numbered holes. Align one end of the leather strap beneath holes 1 and 2. With an awl, mark the holes onto the leather strap and punch the holes with a leather hole punch.

16. Thread the needle with 12 inches (30.5 cm) of thread.

17. Enter the needle into hole 1 of the strap and the cover **(B)**. Draw the thread to the outside of the cover, leaving a 2-inch (5.1 cm) tail on the inside.

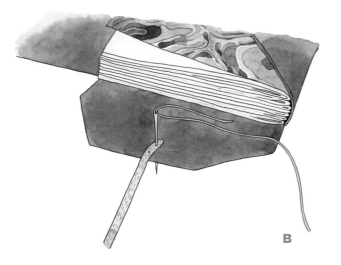

B

18. Enter the needle into hole 2 of the cover and draw it to the inside through hole 2 of the strap **(C)**. Repeat the stitch so there are two threads connecting holes 1 and 2 on the outside of the cover. Enter the needle into hole 3 from the outside of the cover **(D)**.

19. Repeat steps 18 and 19 for holes 3 and 4 and holes 5 and 6.

20. To close the book, fold the rectangular flaps one over the other, covering the text block. Wrap the plain angled flap over and then bring the flap with the strap over it. Secure the book by wrapping the strap twice around the book and tucking the end of the strap beneath the wrapped straps. You can trim the end of the strap to your preferred length.

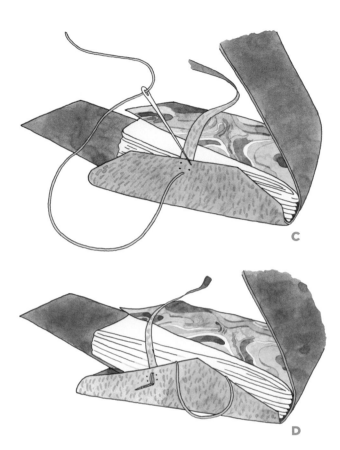

C

D

JOURNALING INSPIRATION

Make an elemental recipe using your own life experiences as ingredients. Provide some instructions on how you have combined these experiential ingredients to create the unique magic that is "you."

JOURNALS
for EVERYDAY
VIRTUES

BEAUTY

LIFE IS A MYRIAD OF EXPERIENCES—SOME HIGH, SOME LOW, AND MANY IN BETWEEN. LET THIS BUTTERFLY-INSPIRED JOURNAL INSPIRE YOU TO FIND BEAUTY AND FLIGHT IN YOUR PERFECTLY IMPERFECT LIFE.

Finished Dimensions

4¼ × 4 × 2 inches (10.8 × 10.2 × 5.1 cm)

Binding Technique

Long-stitch variation (page 19)

What You Need

Basic Bookbinding Toolkit (page 11)

Bookbinding thread in colors of your choice: two 10-inch (25.4 cm) lengths for the butterfly's antennae and the leather tie, 18 inches (45.7 cm) for the weaving on the butterfly's body

Bookbinding thread in second color of your choice, 80 inches (203.2 cm) for binding and butterfly's wings

54 sheets of text-weight paper, 4 × 8 inches (10.2 × 20.3 cm)

9 sheets of handmade paper in colors of your choice, 4 × 8¼ inches (10.2 × 21 cm)

Cardstock for templates

2- to 4-ounce leather (0.8 mm to 1.6 mm thick): 4½ × 13 inches (11.4 × 33 cm), for cover and ¼-inch (6 mm) wide leather strap, 26 inches (66 cm) long, for tie

Optional: Try dying the handmade sheets of paper yourself (page 117)!

MAKE THE SIGNATURES

1. Divide the text-weight sheets into groups of 6 sheets each. With a bone folder, fold each group into a signature measuring 4 × 4 inches (10.2 × 10.2 cm). You will have a total of nine signatures.

2. Place one of the handmade papers horizontally on your table. Position a signature on top of the handmade paper, aligning the fore edges of the papers.

Wrap the other edge of the handmade paper around the signature, folding any excess around the spine of the signature. Repeat for all remaining signatures.

3. Stack the wrapped signatures into a text block **(A)**.

A

PUNCH HOLES IN THE SIGNATURES

4. Make a signature punch guide on cardstock from Template 1.

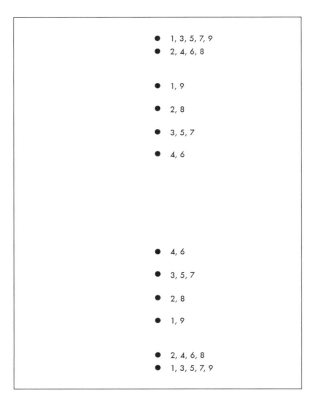

● 1, 3, 5, 7, 9
● 2, 4, 6, 8

● 1, 9

● 2, 8

● 3, 5, 7

● 4, 6

● 4, 6

● 3, 5, 7

● 2, 8

● 1, 9

● 2, 4, 6, 8
● 1, 3, 5, 7, 9

Template 1: Signature Punch Guide, 3 × 4 inches (7.6 × 10.2 cm). Shown at full size.

5. Fold the punch guide in half vertically so the dots are along the fold. Pull the bottom signature from the text block. Nest the guide into the center of signature 1 and punch all sewing stations labeled 1. Remove the guide and stack the punched signature to the left of the text block.

6. Pull the next signature (signature 2) from the bottom of the text block. Nest the guide into the center of the signature and punch all the sewing stations labeled 2. Remove the guide and stack the punched signature on top of the previously punched signature.

7. Continue pulling each signature from the bottom of the text block and punching the sewing stations labeled with the station number corresponding to the signature. After each signature is punched, place it on top of the stack of punched signatures.

8. Once you have punched all nine signatures according to their numbers, you will have formed a text block with a pattern that matches the sewing stations on Template 2 (with all but sewing stations A1, A2, and A3 punched).

PUNCH THE COVER

9. Create a punch guide from Template 2. Be sure to include the row and station numbers around the rectangle. They will be used for reference as you're sewing.

10. Place the leather cover horizontally on your surface with the back side facing up. With a ruler and pencil, make two marks 4 inches (10.2 cm) from the short edge of the cover at your left: one on the long top edge and one on the long bottom edge of the leather.

11. Align the long edge Template 2 on the pencil marks, with the template's arrow pointing upwards.

12. With an awl or a pen, mark all sewing stations onto the spine of the cover, including the ones labeled A1, A2, and A3. Punch out the holes with a ³⁄₁₆-inch (4.8 mm) punch.

ASSEMBLE THE BOOK

13. Begin by sewing the antennae of the butterfly onto the binding using the sewing stations labeled A1, A2, and A3 on Template 2. Position the leather cover with the back side facing up and the short edge facing you. The sewing stations labeled A1, A2, and A3 should be on the left side of the spine.

14. Thread a needle with 10 inches (25.4 cm) of binder's thread in the color of your choice. For example, I chose black thread for both the antennae and the decorative weaving on the body. Starting from the back side of the cover, enter the needle into hole A1. Pull the thread to the front of the cover, leaving a 2-inch (5.1 cm) tail inside the cover.

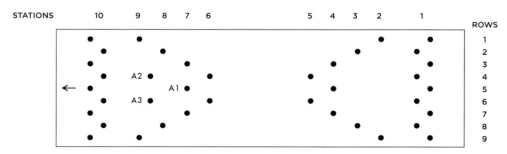

Template 2: Cover Punch and Sewing Guide, 1¼ × 4¼ inches (3.2 × 10.8 cm). Shown at full size.

15. Enter the needle into the hole A2 and pull the thread through to the back side of the cover. Return the needle to A1 and pull the thread to the back of the cover. Repeat this step to create two stitches between holes A1 and A2 for the butterfly's antenna.

16. Draw the needle through hole A1 and pull it to the front of the cover. Create two stitches between holes A3 and A1. Finish sewing by drawing the needle to the back side of the cover.

17. Tie off the ends with a square knot. Trim ends to ⅛ inch (3 mm) **(B)**.

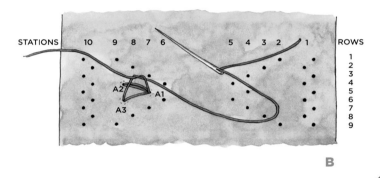

B

18. Thread a needle with 80 inches (203.2 cm) of binder's thread in a second color for the butterfly's wings. I chose pink, for example.

19. Begin sewing signature 1: Pull the bottom signature from the text block. Place the signature inside the cover so its fold is near row 1. Starting from the outside of the cover, enter the needle into the station 1 in row 1. Pull the thread into station 1 of the signature, leaving a 10-inch (25.4 cm) tail of thread on the outside of the cover. Continue sewing the

signature with a running stitch until you reach station 9 and draw your thread inside the signature. At station 9, bring the needle back to the outside of the cover through station 2 and draw it inside the signature again at station 9. This will create a second stitch between sewing stations 2 and 9. To finish sewing signature 1, make a running stitch to station 10 and draw the thread to the outside of the cover **(C)**.

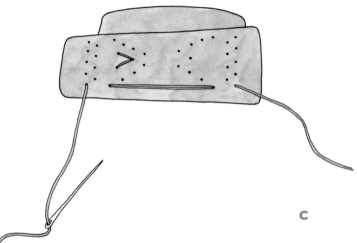

C

20. Pull a new signature from the bottom of the text block and direct-link it to the previous one by guiding the needle into row 2, station 10. Continue sewing signature 2. You will sew two stitches between stations 8 and 3 **(D)**.

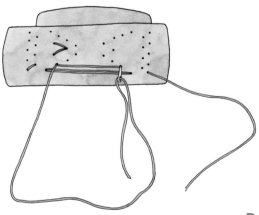

D

21. Continue sewing in this pattern, referring to Template 2 to determine which sewing stations to use in each row. Make sure you double the stitching around the center stations each time. When you reach station 10 in row 9 (the last sewing station of the ninth signature), draw the needle to the outside of the cover and pull the threads taut.

22. To fill in the gaps between the threads at the top and bottom of the rows, place the book in an upright position so the spine is facing you and the needle and thread are hanging from the top right station. Enter the needle at station 10 in row 8. Draw the thread through the cover only and pull the thread taut. You will be making the zigzag pattern at each end of the spine. Enter the needle into row 7 in station 10 and draw the thread back to the outside through the cover only. Continue stitching and filling in the gaps between the stitches **(E)**. Remember to sew through the cover only.

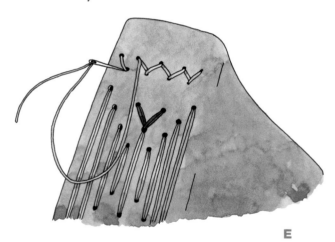

E

23. Once you reach station 10 in row 2, draw the thread to the inside of the nearest signature. Pull the thread taut. Tie the thread off to the thread inside with a square knot. Trim the thread end to ¼ inch (6 mm).

24. Repeat steps 22 and 23 to sew the stations on the other end of the spine.

25. To add decorative weaving to the butterfly's body, thread a needle with 18 inches of thread. Open the book to the center of the fifth signature. Anchor the thread (page 29) near station 4. Enter the needle into station 4 and pull it to the outside of the cover. Pull the thread taut.

26. Close the book and position it between your knees so the spine is facing up. Weave the needle over and under each individual thread on the double stitching in row 5 **(F)**. As you make the weave, use the tip of your needle to pack the stitches so they lie close to one another and form a solid stitching pattern.

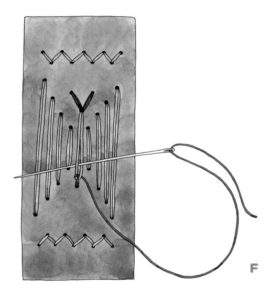

F

27. Once you reach the top of the body, enter the thread into station 7 on the cover and draw the thread to the inside of signature 5.

28. Pull the thread taut and tie off to the stitching inside of the signature (see Tying Off the Binding, page 27). Trim thread ends to ¼ inch (6 mm).

ATTACH THE TIE

29. Thread a needle with 10 inches (25.4 cm) of thread.

30. Punch two holes ½ inch (1.5 cm) apart, starting ½ inch (1.3 cm) from the end of the leather strap. Punch matching holes ½ inch (1.3 cm) from the edge of the wraparound cover **(G)**. Position the cover with the newly punched holes on the back side facing up. Align the holes in the tie with the ones on the cover. The long end of the tie will run outwards from the edge of the cover.

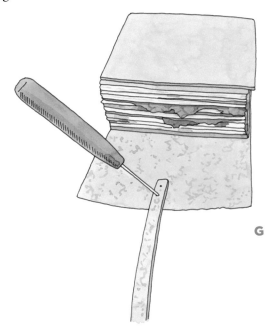

G

31. Enter the needle into the hole of the tie farthest from the cover's edge. Draw the thread through the tie and the cover holes and pull it to the front side of the cover, leaving a 2-inch (5.1 cm) tail on the back side of the tie.

32. Enter the needle into the other hole in the cover. Draw the thread through the tie hole and to the back side of the tie. Repeat the stitch so there are two threads connecting the two holes on the outside of the cover. You should have two threads showing on the front of the cover.

33. Pull the thread taut. Remove the needle and tie the loose thread ends together with a square knot (page 28). Trim the thread to ¼ inch (6 mm).

34. To close the book, wrap the tie twice around it and secure the end beneath the tie on the front cover. If the tie seems too long, pull the end across the spine and trim it where it touches the weaving.

JOURNALING INSPIRATION

Use this book to track your high and lows. Try not to judge your thoughts or words, simply record what comes to you. Challenge yourself to find beauty and gratitude in your most challenging moments. See if you can find appreciation for your flaws—they are, after all, your beauty marks! Record any particular moments of self-transformation or personal growth that you notice over time.

NATURALLY DYED PAPERS

Bring a rainbow of color to your books with these natural dyes made from teas, roots, and other common foods. The dye ingredients create the following colors:

- Red cabbage: pale to bright blue
- Hibiscus leaves: bright pink or purple
- Yellow onion skins: light to dark beige
- Red onion skins: pale bluish gray
- Ground turmeric: golden yellow
- Yerba mate tea leaves: sage green

WHAT YOU NEED

1½ cups (355 mL) water

One or more of the following dye ingredients:

1 cup (500 mL) red cabbage, finely chopped

⅛ cup (30 mL) dried hibiscus leaves

1 cup (500 mL) yellow onion skins, tightly packed

1 cup (500 mL) red onion skins, tightly packed

⅛ cup (30 mL) ground turmeric

⅛ cup (30 mL) yerba mate tea leaves

1-quart (946 mL) saucepan with lid

White or natural-colored paper such as hot-pressed watercolor, cotton rag, mulberry, or lokta paper

Heat-safe shallow baking dish, large enough to fit your paper

Mesh strainer

Measuring cup

Large paper bag

Old towel

Tongs (optional)

Wax paper (optional)

Note: This produces enough dye for up to 5 sheets of 8 × 11½–inch (20.3 × 29.2 cm) paper in each color.

To dye larger amounts of paper, scale the ingredients as follows:

- 6–12 sheets: double the amount of water
- 12–35 sheets: double the amount of water, double the amount of dye ingredient
- 36 sheets: triple the amount of water, double the amount of dye ingredient

Because these natural dyes do not contain additives, expect the paper colors to change over time, depending on the dye ingredient and the amount of light exposure that your pages receive.

continued

Opposite: Paper types, from top to bottom of each stack: 100% cotton watercolor paper, 100% cotton rag from India, heavyweight canvas paper, unbleached mulberry, natural lokta. Dye ingredients used, starting from top left: yerba mate, red cabbage, yellow onion skin, hibiscus, turmeric, red onion skin.

MAKE THE DYE

1. Fill a saucepan with 1½ cups (355 mL) of water.

2. Place your chosen dye ingredient in the saucepan. Cover your pan. Bring your pot to a boil; then simmer on low heat for 15 minutes.

3. Place a mesh strainer over the baking dish. Pour the contents of the saucepan into the strainer over the dish to separate the liquid from the dye ingredients. Let the liquid cool to room temperature. Discard the dye ingredients that were in the strainer.

DYE THE PAPER

4. Place a paper bag or other protection on your work surface to protect it from the dye.

5. Submerge one or multiple sheets of your paper in the dye for five minutes. If submerging multiple sheets, be sure that each side of each sheet is fully exposed to the dye bath.

6. Remove the paper with your hands or with a pair of tongs. The dyes may temporarily stain your skin, but the stains will lighten with soap and water and fade over time.

7. Smooth the papers against a glass window to dry. Place a towel on the windowsill catch any drips. Alternatively, spread out sheets of wax paper on a flat surface and lay your papers out to dry.

8. Repeat steps 1–7 for each dye ingredient you want to use.

9. Once the papers are dry, peel them off the window and use them in your project.

10. Store the leftover dyes in containers in the refrigerator. They will keep up to one week. To dispose of them, pour them down the kitchen drain, taking extra care if your sink is made of porcelain. You can also avoid your sink altogether and use the dye to water an outdoor plant or tree.

Tip: The color of the dye will react differently when in contact with glass or metals, as well as different paper types. Experiment and see what colors you can make!

FAITH

ILLUSTRATE YOUR PERSONAL MYTHOLOGY OR ORIGIN STORY USING
THIS SCROLL. WHEN YOU FIND YOURSELF IN DOUBT, LET IT BE A PLACE
FOR YOUR FOUNDATIONS AND GUIDING PRINCIPLES.

Finished Dimensions

33 × 14 inches (83.8 × 35.6 cm)

What You Need

Basic Bookbinding Toolkit (page 11)

Bookbinding thread, 36 inches (91.4 cm)

1- to 2-ounce (0.4 to 0.8 mm thick) leather,
11 × 9 inches (27.9 × 22.9 cm)

¼-inch (6 mm) wide leather cord, 36 inches
(91.4 cm) long

Heavyweight handmade paper: 25 × 11 inches
(63.5 × 27.9 cm) for scroll and 2 × 11 inches
(5.1 × 27.9 cm) for strip

Wooden dowel or upcycled broom handle,
approximately 1 inch (2.5 cm) diameter and 14
inches (35.6 cm) long

5 flat metal thumbtacks

Carpenter's hammer

MAKE THE SCROLL

1. Place the 2 × 11–inch (5.1 × 27.9 cm) strip of
paper horizontally on your work surface. Fold the
paper in half crosswise so its folded size is 1 × 11
inches (2.54 × 27.9 cm).

2. Using a ruler and pen, you will make five marks
along the center of the folded strip of paper. Make
one mark ¼ inch (6 mm) in from the left edge of the
paper. Repeat for the right edge of the paper. Center
these marks between the top and bottom edges of the
paper. Make the three remaining marks: one in the
center of the paper, one between the left and center
marks, and one between the right and center
marks **(A)**.

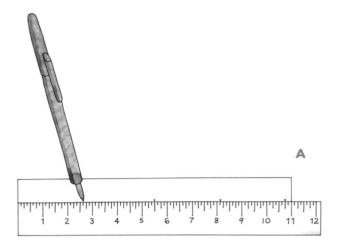

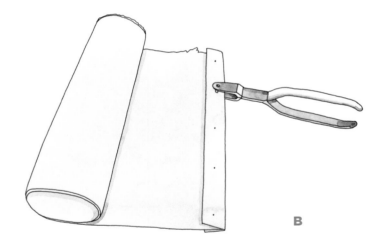

3. Place the heavyweight paper horizontally on your
table. Wrap the folded paper strip around the right
edge. With a hole punch, punch the marks into the
strip and the heavyweight paper at the same time **(B)**.

4. Center the strip and paper layers on top of the
dowel. Press a thumbtack into the center hole and
the dowel. You may need to tap it gently with a
hammer to secure it to the wood. Continue placing
the thumbtacks in the other holes and pressing or
hammering them into the wood, one at a time **(C)**.

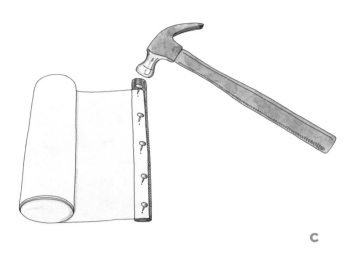

C

Make certain the tacks are placed in a straight line on the wood so the paper will align evenly between the edges of the dowel when rolled up.

5. Place the leather on your table vertically with the back side facing up and the long edges on the left and right. With a ruler and a pencil, make a straight line of marks in ¼-inch (6 mm) increments. The line should be ½ inch (1.3 cm) from the bottom of the leather. Begin the marks ¼ inch (6 mm) from the left edge. Make the last mark ¼ inch (6 mm) from the right edge. Use a leather hole punch to punch the holes.

6. Position the punched edge of leather on top of the loose end of long paper so the holes are ½ inch (1.3 cm) from the edge of the paper. Only the edges of the leather and paper should overlap. Use a pen to mark the holes in the leather onto the paper. Use a paper hole punch to punch the holes.

7. Align the holes of the paper with the holes in the leather. The back side of the leather will be facing up. It should be positioned below the paper with the opposite edge facing away from the scroll.

ASSEMBLE THE SCROLL

8. Thread a needle with the binder's thread.

9. Locate the center hole within the line of holes. Starting from the outside of the paper, enter the needle into the hole and pull the thread through to the underside of the leather. Leave a 4-inch (10.2 cm) tail on the top of the paper. Enter the needle into the next hole and pull it through to the paper side.

10. Continue sewing with the running stitch until you reach last hole. Pull the thread taut.

11. Run the needle back to the previous hole and continue sewing the running stitch to fill the gaps between the threads **(D)**.

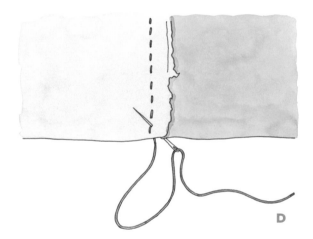

D

12. Once you reach the center, continue sewing the other side of the edge in the same way. At the last hole, begin stitching in the other direction to fill in the gaps between the threads.

13. At the center, tie off the loose threads with a square knot. Trim the ends to 1½ inches (3.8 cm).

TRIM THE LEATHER

14. Position the scroll so the back side of the leather panel is facing down. With scissors, trim the corner off, approximately 1½ inches (3.8 cm) from the edge **(E)**. Place the triangular scrap on the opposite edge to make a matching cut line. Trace the line with a pen. With scissors, cut off the opposite corner using the line.

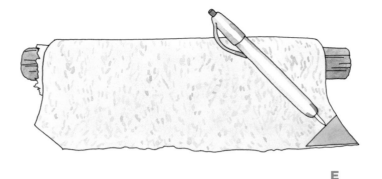

E

ATTACH THE TIE

15. Use a pen to mark a hole 1½ inches (3.8 cm) from the left edge of the leather and 1½ inches (3.8 cm) below the top cut corners. Punch a hole into the leather.

16. Make a knot in the leather cord ½ inch (1.3 cm) from one end.

17. Thread the loose end of the tie through the top side of the hole in the leather. Pull the cord through until the knot rests snugly on the outside of the leather cover **(F)**.

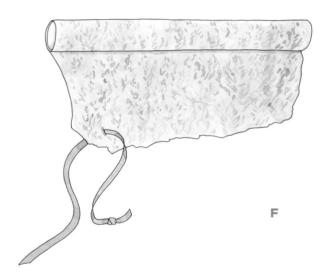

F

18. Roll up the scroll completely. To secure the scroll, wrap the tie down the length of the scroll and then back up again. Tuck the end of the leather cord underneath the wrapped portion.

JOURNALING INSPIRATION

What are the beliefs that help you through challenging times? Or is there a certain myth or origin story that you believe in? Make an illustration of a significant event that shaped you into the person you are. Paint, write, or draw your story onto the scroll so you can refer to it at times in your life when you need a little something to believe in.

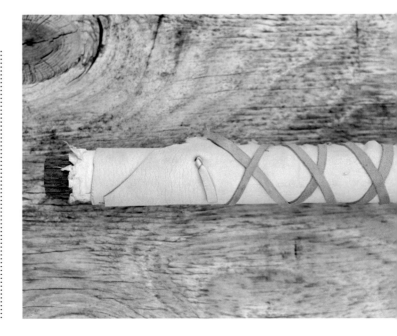

THRIFT

DON'T LET YOUR BOOKBINDING SCRAPS GO TO WASTE. PUT YOUR LEFTOVER STRIPS OF PAPER TO USE WITHIN MINUTES WITH THIS SIMPLE NOTEBOOK.

Finished Dimensions

1¼ × 6 × 1¼ inches (3.2 × 15.2 × 3.2 cm)

Binding Technique

Wrap binding, instructions below

What You Need

Basic Bookbinding Toolkit (page 11)

Bookbinding thread, 54 inches (137 cm)

75 sheets of text-weight paper, 1¼ × 11 inches (3.2 × 27.9 cm)

MAKE THE SIGNATURES

1. Stack the sheets into one pile. Jog all the edges of the sheets to create an even text block.

ASSEMBLE THE BOOK

2. Position the text block horizontally. Take one end in each hand and fold them together to create a V-shaped fore edge. Jog the folded text block on one side to even out the pages. Take hold of the fold securely with one hand.

3. In your other hand, draw the bookbinding thread into the fold between the pages so that the halfway point of the thread is 1¼ inch (3.2 cm) below the fold (A). Pinch the thread at this point with the thumb

that is holding the paper together. Use your other hand to tightly wrap one end of the thread around the entire text block. Wrap evenly until there is a 2-inch (5.1 cm) tail remaining.

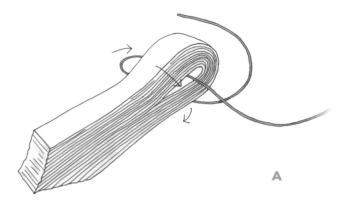

A

4. Pinch the tail under your thumb. With the other hand, take hold of the long thread and evenly wrap the thread around the fold in the opposite direction until a 2- to 3-inch (5 to 7.6 cm) tail meets the first tail.

5. Securely tie the tails together with a square knot. Trim ends to ¼ inch (6 mm).

Tip: Increase your thriftiness and experiment with all sizes of scraps, though be sure that all pages used in a single project are the same dimension.

JOURNALING INSPIRATION

Set this book beside your bed to jot down ideas that arrive in the middle of the night, leave it in your kitchen for shopping lists, or hang it near your door for visitors to leave a greeting when no one is home. To remove a page, fold the top sheet ½ inch (1.3 cm) below the binding and gently tear off. Use the binding as a pencil holder by placing a short pencil in the hole between the fold and the wrapped thread.

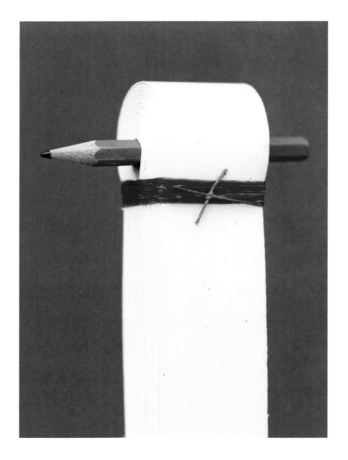

VITALITY

COLLECT YOUR FAVORITE HOMEMADE ELIXIRS, TONICS, AND
SELF-CARE REMEDIES IN THIS LOOSELY BOUND RECIPE BOOK.

Finished Dimensions

3½ × 4½ × 2 inches (8.9 × 11.4 × 5.1 cm)

Binding Technique

Side-stitch variation, instructions below

What You Need

Basic Bookbinding Toolkit (page 11)

50 sheets cardstock, 4¼ × 3⅜ inches
(10.8 × 8.6 cm)

2 wooden boards, 3½ × 4½ × ¼ inches
(8.9 × 11.4 × 6 mm) each

Two ⅛-thick (3 mm) leather cords, 6 inches
(15.2 cm) long each

Scrap wood board, approximately 5 × 5 × 1 inches
(12.7 × 12.7 × 2.5 cm)

³⁄₁₆-inch (5 mm) paper hole punch

Handheld drill or drill press with a ³⁄₃₂-inch
(2.4 mm) wood bit

Dust mask

Safety glasses

Note: I advise being in a well-ventilated area and
using a dust mask for at least the drilling portion
of this project in order to avoid breathing in
sawdust.

Template 1: Signature and Hole Punch Guide, 4½ × 2 ¾ inches (11.4 × 7 cm). Shown full size.

PUNCH HOLES IN THE PAGES

1. Make a punch guide from Template 1 using the cardstock and the paper hole punch.

2. Arrange the 50 sheets of cardstock into a stack.

3. Pull the top sheet from the stack. Position the guide on top of the sheet so the top edges align and the edges of the sheet are centered between the dotted lines. With a pencil, mark the holes onto the sheet. Use the paper hole punch to punch the marks.

4. Use the top sheet as a guide to punch the remaining papers, one to four pages at a time.

MAKE THE COVER

5. Position the guide on the front cover, aligning the top and side edges. With a pencil, mark the center of both holes onto the cover. Repeat for the back cover.

6. Move to a well-ventilated work area, and put on a dust mask to protect your lungs from dust and safety glasses to protect your eyes from dust.

7. Place one of the boards on the piece of scrap wood. With the drill, make holes through the two marks on the cover board. If using a handheld drill, make sure to hold it upright at a 90º angle to the work surface while drilling so the holes are straight. Repeat for the remaining cover board.

8. Dust off the boards and remove your mask. Return to your normal work area.

ASSEMBLE THE BOOK

9. Nest the text block between the cover boards so all holes align.

10. Make a knot ¼ inch (6 mm) from the end of one of the leather cords.

11. Enter the loose end of the cord into one of the bottom cover holes and draw the cord through the text block and to the outside of the top cover. Pull the cord taut. Repeat this step to thread the remaining cord through the other station **(A)**.

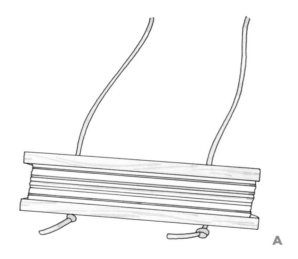

A

12. Gently open the book to the center page. This will cause the cord to loosen and create slack in the binding, which will allow the book to stay flat when open.

13. Lightly close the top cover. With a pencil, mark the cords at the point where they meet the outer edge of the cover holes, then pull the cords taut. Make sure the marks are equal distances on each cord. Place the final knots at the pencil marks. With scissors, trim the ends to ¼ inch (6 mm).

JOURNALING INSPIRATION

Make a collection of your favorite cocktails or DIY self-care products. Alternatively, you can log memorable dining experiences or keep prized family recipes.

PURITY

WHEN LIFE FEELS OVERLY COMPLICATED, LET THIS SIMPLE, FRESH, AND ELEMENTAL BOOK GET YOU THINKING CLEARLY AGAIN. WITH WATER-RESISTANT PAPER, YOU CAN WRITE IN THE RAIN, OR WHILE YOU SOAK IN THE CLAW-FOOT TUB.

Finished Dimensions

3 × 2½ × 1 inches (7.6 × 6.4 × 2.5 cm)

Binding Techniques

Chain stitch (page 21)

What You Need

Basic Bookbinding Toolkit (page 11)

Bookbinding thread, 50 inches (127 cm)

36 sheets of text-weight water-resistant paper, 4 × 5½ inches (10.2 × 14 cm)

Flat stones or tiles, 2½ × 3 inches (6.4 × 7.6 cm)

Electric drill with a 2.55-mm diamond cylinder drill bit

Water tub or sink

Safety glasses

Dust mask

Towel

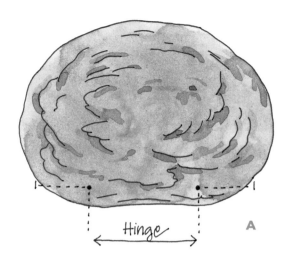

MAKE THE COVER

1. Visit a nearby river to source flat stones that are roughly ½-inch (1.3 cm) thick. If you do not have stones like this in your area, purchase slate tiles from a hardware store or online retailer.

2. Mark two holes for drilling approximately 1½ inches (3.8 cm) apart on the spine of one stone. The holes should be ¼-inch (6 mm) from the edge **(A)**. To make identical marks on the other stone cover, fit the stones together and mark matching holes.

3. Fill the water tub or sink with enough room-temperature water to fully submerge the stones.

4. Fit an electric drill with a diamond cylinder tip. Put on your safety glasses and dust mask. Fully submerge one of the stone covers beneath the water by holding it firmly in one hand. With the drill set on medium-high speed in your other hand, carefully drill through each hole, working from the outside in. Make sure the stone and drill tip remain submerged so the stone dust does not become airborne—you don't want to inhale it. Do practice caution to submerge only the tip of the drill beneath water to avoid risk of shock or damage to the drill. Drill the remaining stone cover. Dry both covers with a towel.

MAKE THE SIGNATURES

5. Divide the paper into nine stacks of four sheets each. Fold each stack into a signature that measures 4¼ × 2¾ inches (10.8 × 7 cm).

6. To make a template for the signatures, place one signature on your work surface and align the holes of one cover with the folded edge of the signature. To create a cutting guide, trace the contour of the stone with an awl, using enough pressure to leave a mark.

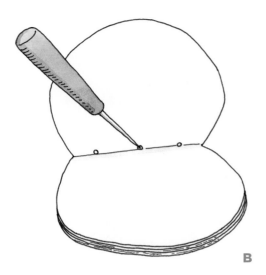

B

7. With scissors, cut along the guide you created on the signature; this will be your tracing guide for the remaining signatures. Align the fold of this guide signature to the fold of the remaining signatures and gently trace the contour with an awl, working with each signature one at a time.

8. Using scissors, cut each signature along the outline as smoothly and accurately as possible.

PUNCH HOLES IN THE SEWING STATIONS

9. To mark the sewing stations, align the inner fold of one signature to one half cover and, with a pencil, lightly mark the two holes onto the inner fold of the signature. For the center hole, find the center point between the other two marks. Pierce each of the three marks with an awl. The interior folded sheet of this punched signature will serve as a punch guide for the remaining signatures.

10. Nest the punch guide within each signature and carefully punch the holes **(B)**. When you're finished, return the punch guide to the interior of the signature from which it came.

ASSEMBLE THE BOOK

11. Line up all the signatures into a text block, making certain they all face the same direction. Beginning with the top signature and the leftmost sewing station, sew the text block together using the chain stitch binding method. Use true kettle stitches to link the top and bottom sewing stations of each signature together. Be sure to leave at least 12 inches (30.5 cm) of loose thread at the first and final sewing stations for attaching the covers.

12. Attach the covers (page 24). Finish by tying off the threads in the inside of the nearest signature (page 27).

One way to change your life is to let go of things or habits that no longer serve you. Make a list of the things you are ready to leave behind. Take a moment to imagine yourself living a simpler lifestyle. What does it look like? How does it make you feel? Use your notes to inspire you to create the change you would like to see in your life.

REVERENCE

WITH THIS ALTAR BOOK, HONOR THE THOUGHTS, IDEAS, AND
WRITINGS THAT ALIGN WITH YOUR HIGHEST BELIEFS.

Finished Dimensions

5½ × 7½ × ¾ inches (14 × 19 × 2 cm)

Binding Techniques

Chain stitch (page 21) variation with French
   stitches (page 23)

What You Need

Basic Bookbinding Toolkit (page 11)

Bookbinding thread, two 70-inch (178 cm)
   lengths

2 binder's boards, 6 × 8 × ¹⁄₁₆ inches
   (15.2 × 20.3 ×1.6 mm)

42 sheets text-weight paper, 5½ ×
   8½ inches (14 × 21.6 cm)

Cardstock for template

2 pieces of lightweight cotton cloth, 5¾ ×
   8 inches (14.6 × 20.3 cm)

4 pieces of lightweight cotton cloth, 3 ×
   8 inches (7.6 × 20.3 cm)

Fabric paint markers

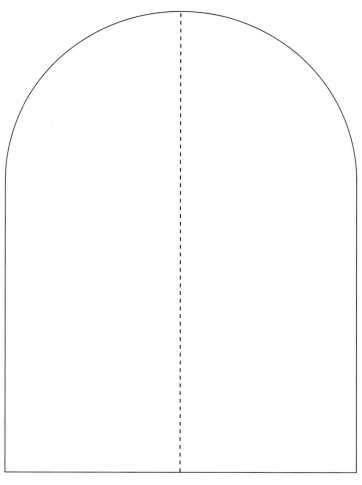

*Template 1: Cover Guide, 5½ × 7½ inches
(14 × 19.1 cm). Enlarge template 150%.*

MAKE THE COVERS

1. Make a cover guide from Template 1 using cardstock.

2. Center the guide on one of the cover boards. Use a pencil to trace the outline of the guide onto the board. With scissors, cut out the shape along the outline. Repeat for the remaining cover board, using the cutout board as a cutting guide.

3. Cut Template 1 in half along the dotted line. With a pencil, trace the long edge of a half of the cover template along the centerline of a cover board. Cut the board in half along the pencil mark. You should now have two half boards of equal size and one complete board.

4. Protect your work surface with wax paper. Using a glue brush, lightly coat one side of the complete board with glue. Center the glued side of the board over one of the 5¾ × 8–inch (14.6 × 20.3 cm) cloths. Press the board onto the cloth, smoothing any creases with a bone folder. Repeat for the other side. Take care to not glue the edges of the cloth to allow them to naturally unravel. With scissors, trim the cloth ¼ inch (6 mm) from the edge of the boards **(A)**. Set aside to dry for about 5 minutes.

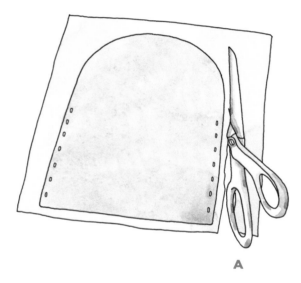

A

5. Repeat step 5 to glue each side of the two half boards using the four smaller pieces of cotton cloth. If needed, use your fingers to fray the edges of the cloth that hangs from the sides of the board.

6. Decorate the cloth boards with fabric markers with simple outline arched lines. Include symbols that are meaningful to you. Set aside to air dry, approximately 10 minutes or until dry to the touch.

MAKE THE SIGNATURES

7. Divide the text-weight paper into 14 groups of three sheets each.

8. With a bone folder, fold each group into signatures that measure 2¾ × 8½ inches (7 × 21.6 cm).

PUNCH HOLES IN THE SIGNATURES

9. Make a punch guide from Template 2 on cardstock. Nest the guide into the center of each signature and, with an awl, punch the holes.

10. Stack the signatures into two text blocks of seven signatures each. Make certain the punched holes are aligned in each signature.

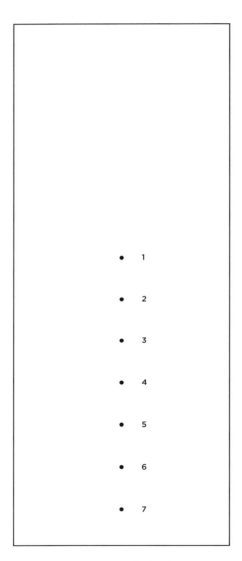

Template 2: Signature Punch Guide, 3 × 7¾ inches (7.6 × 19.7 cm). Enlarge template 133%.

TRIM THE SIGNATURES

11. Position one half of the cover template on top of a signature. Align the straight, long edge of the guide to the loose fore edges of the signature and the curved edge to the fold of the signature.

12. With a pencil, trace the curved portion of the template onto the signature. Make certain the curve starts roughly an inch (2.5 cm) above the punched sewing stations. With scissors, cut the arch out of the signature using the curved outline.

13. Repeat for the remaining signatures. Mark and cut out each signature one at a time. Position the arched signature on each of the remaining signatures, one at a time, using a pencil to trace the arch onto the signatures. Use scissors to cut each signature to size.

PUNCH THE COVER BOARDS

14. Arrange the two half boards on top of the full board. Place the left half board in front of you with the long edge facing right. Position one of the signatures on top of the board. Align the curved edge of the signature with the curved edge of the board.

15. Move the signature ¼ inch (6 mm) from the left edge of the board. Make certain that the bottom edges of the signature and the cover board (not the frayed edges of the cloth) are still aligned. With an awl, punch the top, center, and bottom holes of the signature into the cover board **(B)**.

16. Align the punched cover board to the left and bottom edges of the bottom board. With an awl, mark the holes into the bottom board. Set the top board aside and punch the holes through the bottom board.

17. Repeat steps 14–16 to punch the remaining half cover board and the right spine of the bottom board.

B

ASSEMBLE THE BOOK

18. Prepare the text block for binding. Arrange the seven signatures into a stack. Align the spine of the text block with the spine on the bottom cover. Position the text block and the cover so the spines are facing you. Set the top six signatures to the side.

19. Thread a needle with one piece of binder's thread.

20. Begin binding signature 1: Draw the threaded needle into station 1 (the rightmost sewing station) and pull the thread inside the signature. Leave a 10-inch (25.4 cm) tail on the outside of the cover. Continue sewing with a running stitch until you reach sewing station 4 **(C)**.

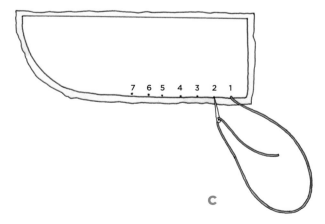

C

21. At station 4, draw the needle to the outside of the signature. Loop the thread twice around the hole in the cover **(D)**. Reenter the needle into station 4.

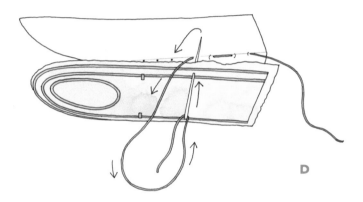

22. Continue sewing with a running stitch until you reach the last sewing station. Repeat the previous step to attach the signature to the cover at station 7.

Tip: As you sew along the spine of the cover, use the tip of your needle to tuck the frayed edges of the board between the cover and the first signature to make sewing easier and give your book a neater appearance.

23. Pull a new signature from your text block and direct-link it to the previous one by guiding your needle into the nearest sewing station.

24. Begin binding signature 2: Draw the needle into station 6 and pull the thread to the outside of the signature. Make a French stitch by wrapping the thread once around the running stitch of the previous signature; then enter the needle into station 5 and pull the thread back inside the signature.

25. Continue to station 4 and pull the thread to the outside of the signature. Link to the previous signature with a chain stitch (page 21). Reenter station 4.

26. Continue to station 3 with a running stitch. Link to the previous signature with a French stitch between stations 3 and 2. At station 1, link the thread to the tail of the first signature with a square knot.

27. For signatures 3 through 6, continue sewing in this pattern: Link to the previous signature with a French stitch between stations 2 and 3 and between stations 5 and 6, with a chain stitch at station 4, and linking true kettle stitches at stations 7 and 1.

28. For signature 7: Continue sewing using the pattern described above with the following exception at sewing station 4. At station 4, draw your thread to the outside of the cover and loop around the hole twice. Tighten the thread; then link to the previous signature with a chain stitch **(E)**.

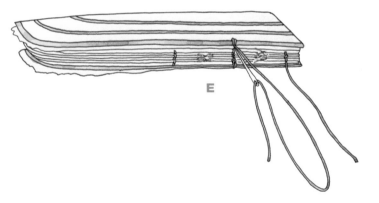

29. Use the loose threads to attach the covers (page 24).

30. Repeat steps 18–29 to sew and attach the covers on the other side of the book. Make certain to orient the spine of the signatures to the opposite spine of the cover board.

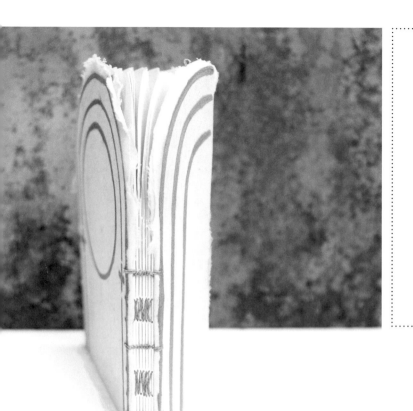

Collect inspiring quotes or excerpts from spiritual texts that resonate deeply with you. Fill the pages with the names of your ancestors and those who you wish to honor and remember. Ask yourself: What is most important to you at this time in your life? Who and what do you live for? What do you wake up for each day? Once you have begun filling the pages, visit your book for inspiration and uplifting guidance.

CREATIVITY

INVITE JOIE DE VIVRE INTO YOUR LIFE WITH THESE GEOMETRIC, COLORFUL, MULTI-SHAPED ARTIST'S JOURNALS.

Finished Dimensions

Triangle: 3½ × 3½ × ¾ inches (8.9 × 8.9 × 1.9 cm)

Half-circle: 2¼ × 4½ × ¾ inches (5.7 × 11.4 × 1.9 cm)

Square: 3 × 3 × ¾ inches (7.6 × 7.6 × 1.9 cm)

Binding Techniques

Chain stitch (page 21)

What You Need

Basic Bookbinding Toolkit (page 11)

Triangle

1 book board, 3½ × 3½ inches (8.9 × 8.9 cm)

4 sheets of canvas paper, 3½ × 3½ inches (8.9 × 8.9 cm)

Bookbinding thread, 45 inches (1.1 m)

15 sheets of canvas paper, 3½ × 7 inches (8.9 × 17.8 cm)

Half Circle

2 book boards, 2½ × 4½ inches (6.4 × 11.4 cm)

Cardstock for template

4 sheets of canvas paper, 2¼ × 4½ inches (5.7 × 11.4 cm)

Bookbinding thread, 45 inches (1.1 m)

15 sheets of canvas paper, 5 × 4½ inches (12.7 × 11.4 cm)

Square

2 book boards, 3 × 3 inches (7.6 × 7.6 cm) each

4 sheets of canvas paper, 3 × 3 inches (7.6 × 7.6 cm)

Bookbinding thread, 45 inches (1.1 m)

15 sheets of canvas paper, 3 × 6 inches (7.6 × 15.2 cm)

Paintbrush

Acrylic paint in colors of your choice

Metallic paint marker

Wax paper

MAKE THE COVERS

1. Prepare the covers for the triangle and half-circle books. To make two triangle boards, use a paper cutter to cut the 3½ × 3½–inch (8.9 × 8.9 cm) board diagonally from one corner to the other. For the half-circle board, create a cover guide from the cardstock using Template 1. Position it on one of the 2½ × 4½–inch (6.4 × 11.4 cm) book boards and use a pencil to trace around the edges. Use sharp scissors to cut out the half-circle shape. Repeat for the other board.

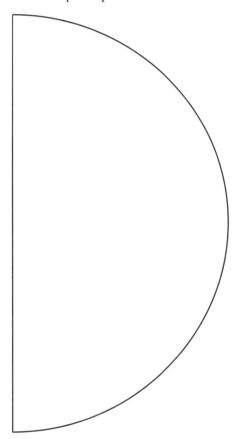

Template 1: Half-Circle Cover Guide, 2¼ × 4½ inches (5.7 × 11.4 cm). Shown at full size.

2. Cover your work surface with wax paper. Choose one of the book shapes and place the cover boards and canvas papers on your work surface.

3. Using a glue brush, coat one side of one of the cover with glue. Press the glued side onto the back side of one of the canvas papers. With a bone folder, press the canvas paper onto the boards and smooth out any air bubbles.

4. Use scissors to trim the excess canvas paper from the edges of the board so all the edges are flush **(A)**. Coat the other side of the board with glue and press it to the back side of another sheet of canvas paper. Again, press and smooth the canvas onto the board with a bone folder and trim any excess canvas from the board.

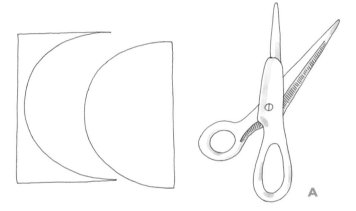

A

5. Repeat steps 3 and 4 for the remaining boards.

DECORATE THE COVERS

6. With the acrylic paint and paintbrush, coat one side of each board with the colors of your choice. Allow the paint to dry, about 10 minutes. Turn the boards over and coat the other sides, then allow to dry.

7. Use a metallic paint marker to color the edges of all the boards. Allow the paint to dry.

MAKE THE SIGNATURES

8. For each shape of book, divide the canvas paper into five stacks of three sheets each. Fold each stack in a signature with the following measurements:
   - Triangle: 3½ × 3½ inches (8.9 × 8.9 cm)
   - Half circle: 2¼ × 4½ inches (5.7× 11.4 cm)
   - Square: 3 × 3 inches (7.6 × 7.6 cm)

9. To shape the signatures for the triangle book, place one of the triangle covers on top of a signature; the folded edge of the signature should align with one of the short edges of the triangle. With an awl, trace the long edge of the triangle onto the signature below. Use enough pressure to leave a mark for a cutting guide. With scissors, trim the signature along the marked line **(B)**. Use this signature as a template to mark and trim the remaining signatures in the same manner.

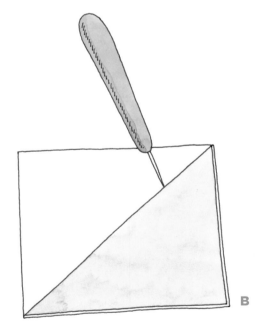

B

10. To shape the signatures for the half-circle book, place one of the half-circle covers on top of a signature; the long edge of the cover should align with the fold of the signature. With an awl, trace the outline of the curved edge of the circle onto the signature below. Use enough pressure to leave a mark for a cutting guide. With scissors, trim the signature along the marked line. Use this signature as a template to mark and trim the remaining signatures in the same manner **(C)**.

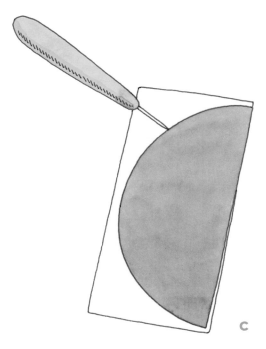

C

11. Place the signatures inside the covers to make sure all edges are flush. Trim any overhanging edges off individual signatures using scissors.

PUNCH HOLES IN THE SIGNATURES AND COVER BOARDS

12. Make a punch guide for one of the books. Pull one signature from the text blocks. Using a ruler and pencil, make a mark ½ inch (1.3 cm) from the top and bottom edges along the center fold line. Mark the center of the fold line as well. You will have a total of three marks.

13. Use an awl to punch all the marks in the signature.

14. Pull the center sheet from the signature. This folded sheet will be your punch guide for the remaining signatures. Nest the punch guide inside each of the remaining signatures and punch the sewing stations with an awl.

15. Return the punch guide to its original place inside the first punched signature. Line up all signatures within their covers.

16. Choose a signature and lay it on top of its cover board, aligning the spine, top, and bottom edges. Shift the signature spine ¼ inch (6 mm) from the spine edge of the cover board.

17. Use an awl to mark the position of the top and bottom sewing stations of the signature onto the board. Set the signature aside. With the awl, punch through the marks on the cover board **(D)**.

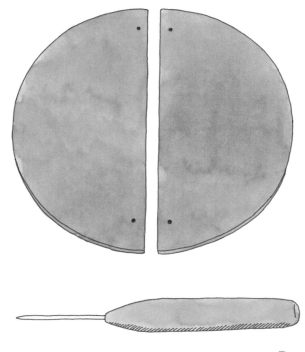

D

18. Lay both cover boards on the work surface. Align the spine edges of the covers so they are touching. Mark matching holes on the unpunched cover, ¼ inch (6mm) from the spine edge. Pick up the board and punch the holes. Place the entire text block within the covers.

19. Repeat steps 12–18 to punch the signatures and cover boards for the other two books.

ASSEMBLE THE BOOK

20. To assemble one of the books, position the book so the spine edges are facing you. Beginning with the bottom signature and the leftmost sewing station, sew the text block together using the chain stitch and use true kettle stitches to link the top and bottom sewing stations of each signature together **(E)**. Leave at least 12 inches (30.5 cm) of loose thread at the first and final sewing stations for attaching the covers.

21. Attach the covers (see page 24). Finish by tying off the threads in the inside of the nearest signature (see Tying Off the Binding, page 27).

22. Repeat steps 20–21 for the other two books.

JOURNALING INSPIRATION

Use these mini books to tune into your unique artistic expression. Experiment by filling the pages with abstract shapes using a rainbow of paint hues. Layer over the painted shapes with metallic paint pens to define the shapes and illuminate your artwork. Allow each page to fully dry before closing the book.

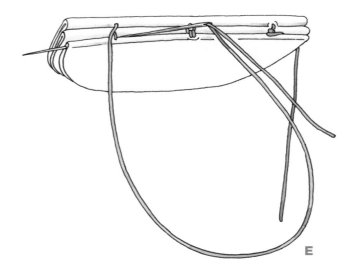

E

BOOKMAKING TERMINOLOGY

AGAINST THE GRAIN, WITH THE GRAIN

Refers to the direction the paper is folded. *Against the grain* is folding the paper at right angles to the grain in the paper. *With the grain* is folding the paper parallel to the grain. See GRAIN.

ANCHORING THE THREAD

A technique used to attach a new length of thread to the inside of a signature with a square knot. The thread is then used for decorative stitching or binding.

CARDSTOCK (COVER STOCK)

A heavy paper used for making templates, usually 80 lb. (120 gsm).

CASE

A book cover that protectively encases or wraps around the text block. The case is made separately from the text block and is attached later.

DIRECT LINK

A technique used to link signatures that involves drawing the thread directly from one station into an adjacent station of the nearest signature without making a knot.

END SHEETS

The sheets of paper (often decorative) located between the cover and the text block.

EXPOSED SPINE

A bound spine that is not covered with material. Rather, both the text block and the stitching are visible, and the stitching is both decorative and functional to the structure of the book.

FORE EDGE

The outer vertical edge of the pages and covers of a book, opposite the spine edge.

GRAIN

Refers to the direction in which the fibers in the paper lie and is often considered when folding the paper into signatures. See AGAINST THE GRAIN, WITH THE GRAIN.

HEAD

The top page edges or the top of the spine. See also TAIL.

JOG

To firmly hold a group of sheets or signatures together and knock one edge against a hard, flat surface to align the individual edges.

LEAF

A single sheet of paper. One leaf has two pages.

LINK

See DIRECT LINK.

LIVE EDGE

The rough, often organically shaped edge of a piece of leather or wood that is left unfinished. Also called *raw edge.*

PAGE

One side of a leaf. The number of leaves multiplied by two equals the number of pages in a book. See SHEET.

PAMPHLET

A booklet made of one signature or section.

SEWING STATIONS

The pierced or punched holes along the folds of a signature that hold the thread of the binding.

SHEET

The full size of the paper before it is folded at the midline.

SIGNATURE, SECTION

Two or more sheets of paper stacked and folded as a group. Technically, the word *signature* is a term used by printers, while *sections* is sometimes used by binders. In this book, I use the term *signature.*

SPINE

The bound edge of a book where the text block is stitched together with thread: the backbone of the book. I also refer to the folded edge of the signature as the spine of the signature.

TAIL

The bottom edge of the spine of the book. See HEAD.

TAPES

Thick paper, cloth, or cordage that is placed between one or more sewing stations on an exposed spine and is integrated into the binding to strengthen the structure of the book.

TEXT BLOCK

The total compiled signatures of a book. In this book, this includes the end sheets.

TIE OFF

To complete the binding of the text block by drawing the tails of the thread into the sewing station of the nearest signature and fastening them to the thread inside the signature with a square knot.

RESOURCES

Begin your search for materials and tools at your locally owned art, craft, and thrift shops. Not only will your purchase support the livelihood of local purveyors, but you may also find a quicker, and sometimes less expensive, route to the best product by asking an experienced employee for recommendations. If a local shop doesn't carry what you're looking for, try checking out the following tried-and-true suppliers.

Binding Tools, Threads, and Paper

TALAS
Brooklyn, NY
talasonline.com

HOLLANDERS
Ann Arbor, MI
hollanders.com

JOHN NEAL BOOKSELLER
Greensboro, NC
johnnealbooks.com

MULBERRY PAPER DESIGN AND MORE
Parker, CO
mulberrypaperandmore.com

FRENCH PAPER COMPANY (MADE IN USA)
Niles, MI
frenchpaper.com

Diamond Drill Bits

RIO GRANDE
Albuquerque, NM
riogrande.com

Leather and Leather Craft Tools

HORWEEN LEATHER COMPANY (MADE IN USA)
Chicago, IL
horween.com

TANDY LEATHER
USA
tandyleatherfactory.com

OREGON LEATHER COMPANY
Portland, OR; Eugene, OR
oregonleatherco.com

MACPHERSON LEATHER COMPANY
Seattle, WA
macphersonleather.com

ACKNOWLEDGMENTS

My gratitude–

To my parents and the long line of crafters and makers in my family, known and unknown—you are my source.

To my family, James, Eden, and Natteo, for sharing my love of books, and for enduring my attention away from home while I wrote this one. Thank you for the biggest love I've ever known. And to our little one on the way, you were part of this book too, and we can hardly wait to share this love with you.

To my aunt, Laurie Tangen, for inviting me into your world of arts and crafts when I was a young girl and for showing me how to sew clothes, paint ceramic raccoons, make fruit roll-ups, and everything having to do with making beautiful messes.

To my editor, Elysia Liang, for your brilliant eye, your keen capability in navigating the bookbinding process, and the unwavering kindness and grace you've given me from start to finish of this process.

To production editor Scott Amerman, for your meticulous eye for detail and for organizing all the pieces of this book into a functional "library of projects."

To dear friend and production assistant, Jane Bear (Jane Bear Photography) for your spirited camaraderie and your highly tuned vision, and for helping me bring these projects to life through the lens.

To art directors of Lark Crafts, Jo Obarowski and Lorie Pagnozzi, for making this book as beautiful as the first.

To Alexis Seabrook, for sharing your highly skilled craft with us in the form of the gorgeous new illustrations.

To my bookbinding sister, Anna Jane Gray Morris, for adventuring into collaboration with me, and to all my sisters of the tide for being a constant source of inspiration. Thank you for beaming your practical magic into the world.

To my fellow booklovers and all of you who have attended workshops with me, collaborated with me, and supported my work in any way: Thank you for your honest reflection and for inspiring my journey.

To the stones, the plants, the water, and the bees—this wouldn't be without you.

INDEX

Note: Page numbers in *italics* indicate projects.

ABOUT THE AUTHOR

Erica Ekrem was shaped by the quiet strength of flatlands, by the stories her grandmother told her during the long winters on the South Dakota prairie, and by her mother and father who raised her to be curious and to connect with the fauna and flora of her surroundings. As a young adult, Erica studied art, graphic design, literature, and architecture and spent much of her time in the aisles of university libraries. It was then when she received her first bookbinding lesson, and her path in folk bookbinding began. Her work has been featured in Design*Sponge; *The Royal Society of Literature*; *Cloth Paper Scissors* magazine, and other printed and online publications. In 2015, Erica authored *Bound: Over 20 Artful Handmade Books* (Lark Crafts), and her original clamshell book design, Book of the Sea, was featured in the Metropolitan Museum of Art's exhibition, The Paper Show. Erica currently offers freelance graphic design for small businesses and nonprofit organizations and empowers others through bookbinding workshops and skill shares. She urges her students to embody authenticity, connect to nature, and honor those who have come before. Her handcrafted journal line can be found at *odelae.com*. Erica lives with her family along the tidelines of the Pacific Northwest.